At the Heart of the Universe

The Eternal Plan of God

Peter Jensen

CROSSWAY BOOKS • WHEATON, ILLINOIS

A DIVISION OF GOOD NEWS PUBLISHERS

At the Heart of the Universe

Copyright © 1991 by Peter Jensen

Published by Crossway Books
a division of Good News Publishers
1300 Crescent Street
Wheaton, Illinois 60187

First Australian edition published by Lancer Books, 1991

First British edition published by Inter-Varsity Press, 1994

First U.S. edition published by Crossway Books, 1997

Cover design by Left Coast Design, Inc. / Portland, Oregon

Cover photo by Science Source / L. Cook

First U.S. printing, 1997

Printed in the United States of America

ISBN 0-89107-964-5

Library of Congress Cataloging-in-Publication Data
Jensen, Peter.
    At the heart of the universe : the eternal plan of God / Peter
Jensen. — 1st U.S. ed.
       p.   cm.
    Based upon the Moore Theological College annual lectures,
delivered in Aug. 1990.
    Originally published: Australia : Lancer Books, 1991.
    Includes bibliographical references and index.
    ISBN 0-89107-964-5
    1. Theology, Doctrinal—Popular works. 2. Providence and
government of God. 3. Economy of God.   I. Title.
BT77.J35   1997
231'.5—dc21   97-3289

06	05	04	03	02	01	00	99	98	97
15	14	13	12	11	10	9	8	7	6	5	4	3	2	1

To Christine

Contents

Preface

The opportunity to write this book came when I was invited to deliver the Moore Theological College Annual Lectures in 1990. I had, on previous occasions, attempted to describe in outline the faith of Christians. The Annual Lecture series served as an ideal moment to attempt this task once again in a more defined way. The lectures were delivered in August, 1990, and were received with sufficient warmth to encourage me to publish them. I have not undertaken major revision, and it will be clear to the reader that the book began its life in these circumstances.

To engage on such a venture was a constant reminder to me of how much I owed to others. I am grateful for the confidence of the College in inviting me to take part in the series. My colleagues have provided support and encouragement including their valuable critical comments. I have received important advice from Helen Martin, John Scott and Phillip Jensen who read and commented on the manuscript. Dr Peter O'Brien acted as Principal of the College while I was preparing the lectures, and he and Mary, his wife, have been treasured friends and fellow-workers over a long period. The typing was done in their usual efficient way by Wendy Dahl and Anne Macklin. Most of the writing was done while I was on leave in England, and the fellowship of Donald and Elizabeth Hay and Ken and Phyllis Bennett was of great significance.

Finally, I wish to say how grateful I am to my wife, Christine, and to our family who so willingly supported me through a number of difficulties and were suitably enthusiastic when the work came to fruition.

Introduction

Doctrine means teaching. Christian doctrine teaches us about God and his purposes for the world. It makes a crucial contribution towards helping us fulfil our goal in life: to know and serve God.

Christian doctrine has a poor name, even among Christians. It is regarded as boring, divisive and irrelevant. Such a reputation, however, is a tragedy which impoverishes the churches and hinders their witness to the world. I have written this short book to describe the essence of doctrine and to show its importance and usefulness.

One major barrier to a positive appreciation of doctrine has been the books written about it. Most introductions to the subject are like textbooks. Although it is important that such works be available, their approach fails to motivate the reader to use them for any other purpose than preparation for examinations.

For many ministers, furthermore, 'doctrine' is merely a subject on the syllabus of their college, and on graduation they find little further use for it. Certainly they would not consider preaching doctrinal sermons or insisting that doctrine be included in Christian education classes.

Doctrine is far too vital and interesting, however, to be locked up in textbooks. Properly understood, doctrine makes the Bible more open to us. It makes sense of the Christian faith and helps us understand its implications for thought and action. It shows us how Christianity compares and contrasts with the ideas and values of the society in which we live. It unites Christians in our common faith and enables us to share the gospel more effectively. Best of all, it stimulates our faith and prayer.

In writing this book, I have three types of person in mind: firstly, the believer who needs to understand God better by seeing the whole truth in outline; secondly, the student who will one day be called upon to preach Christian truth and needs both to grasp its coherence and inner relationships, and also to be encouraged to think about its application; thirdly, those who do not yet know God but who wish to explore the essentials of Christian truth as they consider the claims of the Christian gospel.

The business of Christian doctrine is to communicate the truth about God by describing the main themes of the Christian faith: for example, God, Jesus Christ, the Holy Spirit, revelation, the church and the last things. Textbooks on doctrine tend to treat these subjects as a list, without bringing out the connections between them. A graphic portrayal would be like this:

Revelation	God	Creation	Christ	Salvation	Church	Last Things

The order is logical and it begins with the important question of revelation. But the Bible reader finds the approach rather static and senses a remoteness from Scripture even when the Bible is consistently referred to. It is also apparent that philosophical considerations provide the main context for a number of the key discussions.

In this book I have chosen to reverse the order by considering the 'last things' in the first chapter. The advantage of this procedure is that it captures the biblical sense of purpose in God and the corresponding dynamic of history. The gospel by which we first come to know God involves knowing about the last things, and an exposition which reserves its treatment of them to the end does not adequately represent the Bible or what the Bible has to say about the other topics, including revelation. In seeing what God is planning we gain perspective on who he is and what he is doing to fulfil his ends. The doctrine of God is not complete until we see the whole of what he is achieving.

Beginning with the End as revealed by the purposes and promises of God makes better sense of such topics as revelation and salvation. It provides the indispensable context, too, for thinking about the Christian life. It brings out the relationships that exist between Christian doctrines, relationships which throw light on the significance of the individual themes. It does more justice to the concerns of Scripture and its development and helps overcome the sense of remoteness that I have noted. Finally, it makes it more likely that ethical and existential considerations will emerge from the treatment of doctrine rather than philosophical ones.

In graphic terms, the approach is like this (starting at the base of the triangle):

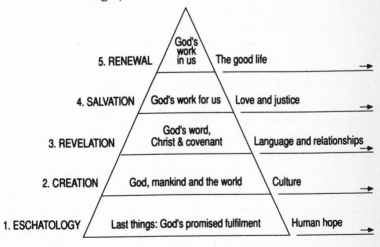

The more conventional titles are given on the left. Within the triangle, the base is given to last things to indicate the way in which God's purposes and promises affect the whole. Christ appears in the centre of the triangle to signify the place he must fill in a statement of Christian faith. The open lines reflect the way in which the themes impinge on one another. On the right are some of the areas of application of doctrine that emerge from the discussions. They do not, however, represent an exhaustive list by any means.

Two last comments about my approach. Firstly, I have written from the standpoint of evangelical theology. The book is not polemical, however, and it comes with the hope that many other Christians can join with evangelicals in this gospel for the sake of our witness to the world.

Secondly, by choice, given the nature of this book, I have chosen not to write in open colloquy with the myriads of historical and contemporary exponents of Christian doctrine. This must not be taken to mean that I am ignorant of their labours or pretend to be unaffected by them. The reverse is the case, and I know that doctrine cannot be attempted without reliance on the work of many other human witnesses to the gracious God who is 'at the heart of the universe'.

To discuss or think about

1 What reactions does the word 'doctrine' arouse in your mind? Why do you think many Christians react to it negatively?
2 What might help us to see doctrine as exciting, as it should be?

PART ONE

Tomorrow, Jerusalem

Occasionally, very occasionally, a whole city will come together to share an inspired moment. Sydney experienced just such a day on 26 January, 1988, when the bicentenary of the arrival of the First Fleet from England was celebrated.

The greatest feature of Sydney is its harbour. The Opera House and the giant 'coat-hanger' bridge, the two most famous of its human landmarks, both derive their splendour from their proximity to the harbour. On a good day – and 26 January was a superb summer's day – the colour and contours of the harbour are dazzling. When a fleet of sailing ships which had made the long voyage from Britain as a re-enactment of the First Fleet arrived in the harbour, it was acclaimed by over one million people who gathered on the shores.

Many participants commented on the spirit of goodwill and harmony in the city that day. Quite appropriately there was an aboriginal protest, but somehow the protest itself was incorporated and even affirmed in the event. The city was proud and sure of itself. In two hundred years a despised and struggling convict colony had become a centre of commerce and culture, a city worth visiting and belonging to.

What the city offers

Cities are like that. People create and live in cities because of the many advantages they offer. Increasingly, the experience of being human is the experience of choosing to live in a city. Consider why this is the case.

The city offers *security*. Once, of course, the city wall kept out thugs and armies. Today we draw together from fear of isolation, of being out of touch when trouble comes, whether that trouble is a rogue human or a crippling disease. It is the rural poor rather than the urban poor who are more likely to die of starvation.[1] It is in the city that the experts gather, that the big hospitals are built, that the security services can be summoned quickly, that justice and government may be found. In the city, nature is domesticated, animals become pets, and the wild becomes a park.

The city offers *companionship*. Living in the remote countryside is all very well for a holiday, but most of us prefer the easier access to friends and family, and the capacity to meet people with the same interests from squash to stamp collecting, that the city provides. The recent cliché for this is 'networking', but before we thought of the word, the city had performed its function of providing us with dozens and dozens of contacts, links, friendships and acquaintances.

The city offers *commerce*. Sociologist Peter Berger has suggested that one of the key features of modern life is the opportunity of choice.[2] The wealth of the city makes these choices possible. The seaport, the stock exchange, the buildings, the banks, the law-courts, the media, the movement of goods for import and export, the thousands of shops, all these things reveal that for most cities barter and exchange are life. Not least is this true of Sydney.

How the city fails

And yet, I have to say that Sydney's great day did not last. Urban people have an urge to be busy, to be doing the next thing, to hasten somewhere else, to attend to the next job on the list. The denizens of the city are taught to be restless. Furthermore, perfection is only ever temporary. In this life there is always a sadness in perfection; we feel that we were made for it, and yet we cannot make it stay. Worst of all, however, the peace and harmony of the day did not last. The city soon returned to its discords, its greed, its loneliness.

Cities offer security, companionship, culture and commerce. How pure and simple is this truth, however? What if the word 'city' also carries with it the idea of criminality, of violence, of fear, of perversion? What if we must hide behind security systems in the city? What if our homes have to be built like castles? What if the city, far from being companionable, was the very symbol in people's minds for loneliness and alienation, where row after row of new slums contain heartbreak, pain, betrayal and brutality? What if people are desperate for intimate and loving human contact? What if the culture of the city was too expensive for its citizens, or corrupting to taste and morality? What if the commercial life of the city was a temple to greed and rapacity, being expressed in contempt for the environment and the ugliness of the architecture?

The Australian playwright David Williamson has portrayed bold and brassy Sydney as 'Emerald City'. Do not think for a moment, however, that more cultured and civilized cities escape criticism. They too have their dark and ugly side. Our discontent is not merely personal and time-bound. It reflects something about the nature of our humanity even in the very place it calls its own, even in the city. For, in the midst of our own brilliant achievements, in the midst of civilization, we are frustrated. The city mocks us by offering so much that pleases and yielding so little that endures; we are still no wiser about what will truly satisfy us, for we do not know who we are, or what we may yet be or how we should live. The city suggests what it is to be human without giving us our humanity; it gives us infinite alternatives without the wisdom needed to choose. It confronts us at every turn with our nobility and our barbarity.

The city of the future

Who are we? What may we be? How should we live? It is true that the Bible begins its answer to these questions with human beings in a park or garden. Among the variety of ways it has of talking about the future, however, one is through the picture of the city; indeed in the Bible's final pages, it is a city which dominates. Here we are shown an image of 'the new Jerusalem', perfectly founded, perfectly proportioned, perfectly inhabited, presented as the place where all human hopes and dreams and aspirations have their fulfilment. In the perspective of the Bible, if we are to understand who we are, if we are to understand the present, we must know about the future. In the symbol of the new Jerusalem and in the other biblical descriptions of the future we will discover clues to our identity, and the path we must tread to genuine fulfilment. Towards the conclusion of part 1, I will turn to the Bible's description of the new Jerusalem, the city which is to come, in contrast with our human cities. Here, something true, deep and eternal may be learned about our noble yet brutish selves.

An idea of what follows

It is my aim in this book to give an outline of Christian doctrine, to show how it fits together, and to relate it to our experience. It is not intended to be a defence of Christianity, arguing the evidences for the truth of God and the gospel, except that to describe doctrine like this does argue the case in itself. I believe that this project will help us grasp the overall message of the Bible and hence assist us as we read it; I believe that it will help us communicate the gospel in our world as we see that it is coherent, relevant and true, and as we can compare it with the alternatives; I believe that it will clear away unnecessary objections to the gospel and help us focus on the real challenges posed by the Christian faith to the unbelieving world.

As you can see, part 1 begins where most doctrine books finish, by talking about the end of the world and the life to come, by considering the new Jerusalem and the other ways the Bible has for describing the future. This may seem like an eccentric procedure. I think, however, that this method brings an important perspective to bear on the whole, and I think that it is close to the heart of the gospel message which began, after all, with the announcement: '"The time has come," he said. "The kingdom of God is near. Repent and believe the good news!"' (Mk. 1:15, NIV). In one sense, God's kingdom is already here. In another sense, we are still awaiting its arrival. As we explore Christian doctrine, the tension between what we experience and what we hope for will be a frequent theme, just as there is tension between our present experience of cities and our hopes for the new Jerusalem.

In this first part, therefore, I will continue to look ahead to God's future. In order to indicate the influence that the future has on our thinking in the first section of chapter 1 I am going to talk about 'The power of the End'.

In the section entitled, 'The beginning of the End', I will indicate what it means to say that God's kingdom is already here. Then in chapter 2 our expectation of the future actions of God will be described under the title 'When the End arrives'. Finally, I will attempt to delineate what God's final plans for us will be like, and what human fulfilment and eternal life will involve, when I speak of 'The essence of the End'.

CHAPTER 1

The End: its power and its beginning

The power of the End

So far I have been using the words 'End' and 'future' as though they mean the same thing, but, of course, that's not true. We all believe that we have some future, be it a matter of days or years. Most of us believe that the world has a future of some sort. But a future as such does not necessarily imply that history has a goal to which it is moving. The word 'End' suggests a goal, and also a purpose to reach that goal.

The end to which the sportsman or sportswoman strives is excellence and competitive success; the end of the soldier at war is peace; the end of study is graduation; the end of pregnancy is birth. Naturally, there is life and striving beyond these ends, other lesser 'ends' along the way, and there are legitimately diverse ends. But the concept of 'the End', the goal, is built into any Christian thought about the future. Christians claim that the flow of time has purpose, and is guided by one who has an End in mind.

The Bible presents God as a purposive Creator and Redeemer, one with an End in view, and it gives us an insight into that End which touches our beliefs and behaviour in fundamental ways, especially providing them with meaning. For, once a person adopts an end, he or she takes the steps necessary to reach the goal. It may be an entirely humble action, like going home after work, which then requires a trip to the bus-stop, the catching of the bus, and a walk to the front door; it may be the vast complications involved in setting up a new business or acquiring a university degree. Whatever it is, the end or goal evokes purpose, and purpose guides us towards the goal with greater or lesser efficiency or motivation. Of this we may be sure, however, that the possession of hope, the longing for a goal, is one of the most powerful stimulants possible to human action. That is true of Marxists who believe that they know where history should go and are prepared to work towards it; it is true of Christians who believe that they know where history will go and are prepared to work in the light of it.

Our own generation is marked more by vagueness and uncertainty of hope than by boldness. 'Hope' has come to mean little more than 'wish', and has been individualized. Yet the absence of hope in the larger sense leaves us prey to what the historian of religion, Mircea Eliade, calls 'the terror of history', the incapacity to make sense of historical events and so draw courage and strength to live now.[1] When we abandon God we are left either with the despair of meaninglessness or with the return to the old myths of constant repetition which helped men and women to escape history.

The fact that Christians can be sure about God, hope and history enables us to speak both to the despair and to the false optimism of our time. The purposes of God give perspective.

Perspective on our own time

Christians know that we are not living in a final and conclusive age, beyond which there is no human consciousness, nothing but the collapse (and re-emergence?) of the universe. We know that this time is not going to be forgotten or ignored; that it will testify about us on the judgment day. Thus we will not over-value this present time, holding on to it with grim determination because it is the only time we have, nor will we undervalue this present time as though what we do with it has no significance at all, as though life is without meaning.

Perspective on our way of life

Our knowledge of God's purposes shapes the way of life that we adopt. Our goals, our values, and our behaviour will conform to the goal which we know that God has. By showing us what will endure, he shows us what to value. By showing us the vital significance of today's choices, he shows us the pattern of life to make our own. By showing us the new Jerusalem, he exposes the failures of our human communities and challenges us to change them. There is great practical significance in knowing the End.

Perspective on our doctrine of man

Think, too, what deeper understanding we are given of man through our knowledge of God's purposes for us. It is a fatal defect of secular anthropologies that they have no sure insight into the future. We can learn much from others about man, but since they do not know the end of man, they cannot give us that true assessment which will sustain and nourish our life here. They cannot respond to the question 'What is man for?' that Christianity supplies an answer to. Economic man, sociological man, psychological man, can make little progress here. An anthropology which assesses man in the abstract, removing us from the historical process, even if it does not make the mistake of also abstracting us from society, will present a static, two-dimensional picture. It cannot pass judgment on what really matters in life. What it means to be human can be judged only by what we know of humanity's true fulfilment.

Perspective on God

There is a connection here, too, with how we think of God. Much can be gained in understanding lions by capturing one, killing it, classifying it, dissecting it and minutely examining it. The living, working lion, however, will yield information that the dead specimen cannot. In our approach to knowing God, it is good to start at the End because we are seeing here the great and purposive Lord of all things. As we see what he plans to do and how he plans to achieve his goal, we see more clearly who and what he is.

Perspective on the scope of doctrine

We are being reminded here of the interrelatedness of Christian doctrine, that it is more like a connected story than a set of systematic assertions. Although we may see fit to study it under headings such as God, Man, Christ, Church, Holy Spirit, we need also to remember that the whole story penetrates and enlightens our appreciation of the individual parts. In short, I am starting at the End because of the power of the End to illuminate the present and to reveal the truth about God.

In the discussion so far I have assumed that the End is in the future. But, in addition to the reasons I have given for studying the End first, there exists an even more basic point: from the Bible's point of view, the End has already arrived. There is a sense in which we are living with and in the End, whether we like it or not. To understand the End that will be, we must understand the End that already is. We turn, therefore, to the theme of Jesus' preaching; the kingdom of God. We turn, in fact, to 'The beginning of the End'.

The beginning of the End

Jesus was a prophet of the End: 'The time is fulfilled,' he preached, 'and the kingdom of God is at hand; repent and believe in the gospel' (Mk. 1:15). According to Mark, this simple message was 'the gospel of God' (Mk. 1:14).

Jesus announced the coming of the kingdom of God. For Jesus and his hearers, God's kingdom is not a place but an activity. It is God's rule. Although it was 'at hand' in one way, there were also three senses in which this rule or kingdom was already a reality in Jesus' life.

The existing reality of God's kingdom

First, there was God's general sovereignty. As Creator of this universe, he is its sustainer and ruler; he controls it, from the mightiest of its stars to the tiniest of its plants and animals and physical elements. This was a reality for Jesus.

Second, there was God's rule over Jesus himself. He was uniquely the servant of the Lord, living, unlike us, as the obedient servant of God's rule because God is the rightful Lord of our race. We have disputed and repudiated God's right to rule over us. Having freed ourselves from the rule of God, we have become ignorant of God. We build our flawed and unsatisfying cities. Jesus Christ, however, lived under God's rule. This was a reality for Jesus.

Third, there was God's rule over his special people. As ruler of the world and its history, God chose and created a family, a people, a nation, to be in a unique contact with him, intended to reflect the proper relationship between God and man. The nation was Israel, and its life was meant to be one of service to the Lord God, a service in which it frequently failed. It was, however, also the recipient of the promises of God. These promises indicated that a future day would come when God would decisively disperse his enemies, reassert his rule, and introduce a new age of righteousness. This was the goal or End of history, and it was what Jesus was announcing: 'The kingdom of God is at hand.'

For Jesus to announce the kingdom of God was not, then, to say that God's rule did not exist until that moment. It was to say that a new stage was about to begin, that the history of the world had now moved to the point of crisis, of action, of its End. It was to announce a new era. It is no wonder that he urged his hearers to capitulate to God's existing rule at once through repentance and faith before the day arrived and they would be overthrown.

The old age continues

To say all this is to raise the question of how good a prophet Jesus was. If one thing is clear to us it is that the rule of God in its decisive form has still not come, nearly two thousand years after our Prophet spoke. His gospel was good, but his news seems false. The world maintains its pain, its evil, its mystery as far as we are concerned; indeed the twentieth century may be the worst epoch yet. There are not lacking those who will tell us that the Jesus experiment is a failure, that nothing has happened. Here, however, is where we must discern the meaning of history as Jesus and the Bible expound it. Our present era is marked by tension between what has come and what is yet to come. To deny the tension is to misunderstand both history and the contemporary moment. The present tension is not unexpected, it is part of what he predicted.

On the one hand, Jesus expected that history would continue. Whether Jesus and his disciples believed that it would be all finished within the near future, or run on as it has over two thousand years so far, is not important. Jesus, in fact, refused to be drawn on that point. What he did endorse, however, was the insight that God remains in control, that the sufferings of history do not count against that control. He saw within the historical experience that all of us pass through certain 'signs of the times' arising from the providential care of God. These signs would function as reminders that God is in charge of history and that it has a terminus. Jesus spoke of nations rising against nations, of wars and rumours of wars, of false Christs and false prophets with signs and wonders, of earthquakes and famines (Mk. 13:6, 8, 22).

The very ordinariness of these signs has frustrated many, but it is the clue to their usefulness. The 'signs' are the ordinary events of history that testify to God's judgment. They are not intended to act as a sort of map to the future, as though the followers of Jesus were being given special advanced information. The bizarre attempts to calculate the date of the End have disfigured Christian history, obscured the gospel and have reflected a misunderstanding of the Bible itself. The function of the signs is to stimulate both patient endurance and readiness for the End, not to satisfy curiosity. The judgments of God in history constantly remind us of the judgment of God that will conclude history, and prepare us for it. The precise moment of its appearing is not revealed to us, nor is the specific meaning of any particular sign. It is sufficient to know that 'he who endures to the end will be saved' (Mk. 13:13).

But the King has come

Thus, on the one hand, history continues despite the announcement that 'the kingdom of God has drawn near'. On the other hand, though, a vital new thing has occurred, and it is not the same history as it was before. In a key sense, 'the kingdom of God is in the midst of you' (Lk. 17:21). The kingdom has come, as Jesus said it had.

Such a bold claim can refer only to one thing: the entry into our world of Jesus Christ himself. Such is the impact of his coming that the Bible has to describe it as the drawing near of the age to come, the new age beyond the Day of the Lord, the age of the fulfilment of hopes and expectations; it has to say that eternal life has not waited for the judgment day, it has pushed itself into the midst of today's history.

Others are making the same claim. We experience the explosion of 'New Age' religions, and it is believed by many that we are living at the dawn of a new era in which human beings can be happy and fulfilled in new ways. But alert readers of popular literature can only be impressed with the lack of substance in it all and, worse, with its overwhelming egocentricity and lack of moral purpose. It seems remarkably like the new age that we would invent in our worst moments. In the desire for a return to unity with Nature, to significance in a crowded world, to the conviction that we are part of a grand scheme of some sort, the New Age has forgotten the presence of the Old Age. As Mircea Eliade observed about the parallel astrological boom, 'you feel in harmony with the universe and do not have to bother with hard, tragic, or insoluble problems'.[2] But Christianity regards us as living in both ages, and insistently draws our attention to Jesus Christ as the key to an understanding of where and what we are.

The presence of our future
The new age announced in the New Testament has been inserted into time, and the old age and the new run on together. It is the time of two ages. The new age has its foundation entirely through the life, death and resurrection from the dead of Jesus Christ. From his birth to his death he never ceased to be the faithful servant of the Lord, the one who lived under God's rule. Men assassinated Jesus by false witness and crucifixion. In raising him from the death of crucifixion, God has declared himself thoroughly pleased with Jesus. More than that, however, God has declared that he is the representative of all men and women, the first of our human race to be raised, and the pattern and guarantee for the rest of us. He is what humanity, we ourselves, are intended to be. He is what we will become; he is the first citizen of the new Jerusalem.

There is a special sense in which this is so. In the early chapters of the Bible we are told that men and women are made in the image of God, and hence share his stewardship of the created world (Gn. 1:26). As God's rule has been disputed by us, so our capacity to rule the world has been severely limited: that is part of the pain and mystery of being fallen. But Jesus Christ, the one ruled by God and approved by God, has himself, and uniquely, been appointed Lord and Ruler of the world during the time of the two ages. He preached the kingdom of God. Since his resurrection, the message remains the same, but is expressed more precisely as the fact that Jesus Christ is Lord, or Ruler. Men and women everywhere are invited to put themselves under his control.

Ever since the resurrection of Jesus Christ and his ascension to the right hand of God, we have been living in the last days; it has been the beginning of the End. How long this period will last is relatively insignificant; for God, a thousand years is as one day and one day as a thousand years. Should history have 50,000 years yet to run, it would still be the last days. Jesus said that God has planted a seed which will one day be a great tree; he has planted a field where his good plants and the devil's weeds will grow together until he is prepared to sort them out (Mt. 13:24–31).

The Bible does indicate, however, that our journey through history will have a conclusion. We are not allowed to assume that history, or rather the unaided human race working in history, can create a perfect civilization. We cannot build ourselves here on earth an enduring city, a new Jerusalem, a superior London, Sydney or New York which will be fit for humanity to live in. Even more important, we cannot create the conditions that would mean that God would accept us gladly as valid and deserving members of his new age. We cannot be good in this life and, specifically, we cannot be good enough for the next. Thus a definite conclusion is needed, that there may be a definite new beginning.

However, this new beginning cannot be made without the past. It is in human history that decisions are made, values forged, lives lived out that will affect the new age, the age to come. If we cannot build our new Jerusalem here, we ought nonetheless to note that what we do here has a bearing on our experience of the new Jerusalem that is God's gift. It is no part of the Christian ideal to despise the present age and what occurs within it. We record only a tiny fragment of it and call it 'history'; God records it completely and with perfect justice for the sake of the age to come.

We should note that Jesus Christ is at the intersection of the two ages. There can be no doubting his sheer human presence in the old age, born of the Virgin Mary, crucified under Pontius Pilate. But he also represents the new age, the age to come. His death occurs in one, his resurrection in the other, and he shows us the connection between the two. He is the presence of the future, the beginning of the End.

It is worth noting that this approach helps to overcome one of the problems of doctrine. The treatment of the last things in many doctrine books seems like an afterthought. Eschatology is not allowed to impinge on the present, and the main Christian doctrines are detached from eschatology. But when we see that the End has begun, and that Jesus Christ is integral to it, a new coherence emerges. Instead of the treatment of the last things being a mere exercise in predicting future events, it becomes in essence the description of the future of Jesus Christ. To know him as he is revealed in the Gospels is to know the essential truth about the future.

To discuss or think about

1 Why is it important to think about the 'end' of any activity that we are engaged in?
2 Why is it important to understand the End towards which God is working?
3 Jesus announced the coming of God's kingdom. In what ways was this kingdom already a reality in his life?

4 How does his announcement of the kingdom square with the state of the world as we see it? In what sense is the kingdom already present?
5 If the End has already begun, in what sense is it still to come?

CHAPTER 2

The End: its arrival and its essence

When the End arrives

The death and resurrection of Jesus marked the beginning of the End. We now come to the point where we think of the future, when the End comes. The Bible describes this as coming in three stages.

The return of Jesus

First, the Bible promises the return or second coming of Jesus Christ. He will be revealed, and on this occasion, to all the world and in all his glory. The final truth about the universe, that he is its Lord, will be made plain, and every creature will do him homage. His return will be sudden, catching many unprepared, despite the warnings of Scripture, and it will be the decisive inauguration of the next stage in God's history.

The resurrection of all

Second, the Bible promises a general resurrection. The resurrection of Jesus is not only the positive verdict of God on his life and death, it is the pattern for the future of our race. In this respect he is called 'Adam' in the Bible, for, like Adam, he is the founder of a people. The Bible calls him 'the last Adam', the final Adam (1 Cor. 15:45). The race begun by Christ, however, is not new, from new stock; it is the old transformed, and the resurrection of all is the reminder that we are dealing here with continuity as well as newness. It is we ourselves, as whole people, not just some part of us or the memory of us, which goes forward into the new life. Resurrection testifies to this continuity of experience, to the wholeness of what goes beyond death, to the completeness of Christ's victory over death. In the very arena where death has done its worst, in the body, God proposes to achieve his victory for us and in us. A Christianity which does not promise bodily resurrection is vacuous.

That is not to say that we know much about it. In the case of Jesus, the tomb was empty of the body laid in it, but his appearances were characterized by features which suggested a translation into another mode of existence. Paul contrasts the old body and the new as seed to full-grown plant, and warns us that 'flesh and blood cannot inherit the kingdom of God' (1 Cor. 15:50). We are given no information about how the new body we will be given is to be connected with the corrupting body which is laid in the tomb and turns back to the elements from which it came. It is enough to see that Christ was raised and to know that what God has done for him, he will do for all.

The judgment of all

The third stage described in the Bible is judgment. God is referred to in Scripture as the completely righteous judge. His judgments, in which he lifts up some and brings down others, are continuous throughout history. Indeed, the experience of the human race itself testifies to the reality of judgment. In the Bible's terms, our rebellion against God was followed by our expulsion from his presence, and by death. Every death is a reminder of judgment (Rom. 6:23).

On the other hand, the judgments of God have not been final. Over and again he has shown mercy and restraint in the face of human pride and selfishness. The Bible, in speaking of God's patience, however, warns us of a wrath that is 'laid up', and of a day in which the whole of human folly will be displayed.

In talking of Christ's future revelation on earth, the Bible connects it with judgment. He is the appointed judge of the living and the dead. All will appear before Christ's judgment seat, whether believer or unbeliever, and the secrets of all will be revealed. No word, no thought, no deed, no failure will be omitted from scrutiny and testing. All will be rewarded, whether believer or unbeliever, whether blame or praise, for nothing can tarnish the righteousness of this judge. In the final analysis, however, there will be those who have embraced eternal life in this life by faith in the Saviour, Jesus, and there will be those who have not. The first coming of Jesus was divisive; the preaching of the gospel has created division amongst the peoples. Ultimately, his word will be forgiveness or condemnation, and the division will be permanent.

For those who are perishing, responsible for their own condemnation through their unresolved rebellion against God's rule, there is the pain of exclusion from the presence of God in hell for ever; of failure to become what they could have been; of the inconsolable loss of that love that should be at the centre of human life and the sharpness of unrelieved conscience. There need be no doubt that this has been their own choice in not wanting to be ruled by God, but we can hardly think of it without pain and horror. The Bible does not tell us whether there be few or many; it offers us – Jesus himself offers us – the most solemn warnings that we should not be amongst them. It seems odd, given the experience we have daily of the obstinate rejection of the gospel by those in a position to know, and the sufferings that are endured as a result of sin in this present age, that some Christians should so easily doubt the reality of hell. 'The curious modern heresy that everything is bound to come right in the end,' writes Professor J. S. Whale, 'is so frivolous that I will not insult you by refuting it. "I remember," said Dr Johnson, on one occasion, "that my Maker has said that he will place the sheep on his right hand and the goats on his left".[1]

Jesus Christ as the key to the future

When judgment has been passed, the End has truly arrived. But before we turn to thinking about the essence of the End, what God has planned for his people in the new age which is his goal, we ought to note once more that Jesus Christ is the key to it all. It is his word about the kingdom that we began with; it is his word by which we live now; he reigns over this present age; it is his return that is our hope, and that will inaugurate the resurrection and judgment; he is to be the judge; even hell is seen to be the declaration that he does not stand in relationship with those who are condemned. The End of the world (and this will become clearer in the next section) is about Jesus first of all.

It is my chief criticism of those theories which talk of a millennial kingdom after the return of Christ (though not my only one) that they encourage speculation about matters to do with prophecy which do not focus the attention on Christ. Talk of politics, of Armageddon, of the Rapture, of the Tribulation subverts the Christian hope and turns prophecy into little better than soothsaying. Our hope is Christ, and it is to him that we come now as we consider 'The essence of the End'.

The essence of the End

Notions of 'heaven'

In popular speech 'heaven' is the name by which the future of God's people is known, and for the moment I am going to adopt it, though it would be better to speak the language of fulfilment and consummation. In fact, it is a daring speaker who will say much about heaven, since his account of it may turn his audience off! Certainly it seems for many people to be a pallid and unattractive place, an everlasting church service with highbrow music in insipid surroundings, in the company of people with whom you would not normally mix. Some would prefer the endless round of reincarnation; only the mystical few are attracted by the vision of Meister Eckhart, in which the soul 'is nearer to God than the body which makes us human. It is more intimate with him than a drop of water put in a vat of wine, for that would still be water and wine; but here one is changed into the other so that no creature could ever again detect a difference between them.'[2]

This language is vivid, but at least it is elevated. There is also a strand of Christian imagination which sees heaven in rather self-centred individualistic terms, as the place where believers' souls ascend when they die, and where they gaze on God for a timeless eternity, preferably in the company of friends. The Bible, true to its practical nature, is not filled with teaching about heaven, but it does enough to correct and inform all these views and to give us the substantial truth. For what follows the present evil age is not eternity, but the age to come, or eternal life, where the experience described is not so much the absence of time as the quality of relationships in the marvellous time which is to come. Whether 'timeless' is the proper description for eternal life I cannot say, but neither the Bible nor we, in using human language, can escape the time-bound words that we use. Nor should we wish to, for our emphasis needs to fall on God's dynamic purposes and his deeds rather than the static vision of God which has sometimes taken its place.

Jesus Christ our future

If we are to have any understanding of heaven or, better, of God's fulfilment for us, it is by continuing the method of focusing on the future of Jesus Christ. After the judgment he remains our last Adam, our man from heaven, and those whose destiny is heaven are said to be in him, that is, in union with Christ. Being *in* him, whether they die before his coming or pass straight from this life to the next, they are to spend the future '*with* him'. Indeed the most succinct description of heaven is surely Paul's: 'My desire is to depart and be with Christ, for that is far better' (Phil. 1:21). The Lord said to the thief dying beside him on the cross: 'Today you will be with me in Paradise' (Lk. 23:43), reminding the believer that paradise is to be with Christ.

In Christ we are; *with* Christ we shall be; *like* Christ completes our hope. Again and again the New Testament promises that we shall be like him: 'Beloved, we are God's children now; it does not yet appear what we shall be, but we know that when he appears we shall be like him, for we shall see him as he is' (1 Jn. 3:2). Here is the proper climax to the 'image' language of the Bible. At the beginning, we are told, male and female were in the image of God in the garden, ruling over the earth. In the end, we now see, men and women are being reconstituted into the image of the last Adam, the man from heaven, so that with him they may reign. I believe that this begins to fulfil the original purpose of God for man, that we should have dominion under God. In the present Lordship of the man Jesus Christ, who rules the world, we see God's intentions for us come to pass. But the day will come, according to the Bible, when Christ will destroy all our enemies, death included. When that is accomplished, as the representative man he will yield his sovereignty to God the Father, and Christ, on our behalf, will subject himself to God. Finally, once more and properly, God will be everything to everyone.

In such a picture of the End, we see the maturing of God's purposes; it completes and transcends the original picture in the Garden of Eden. We see God's rule re-established over an unruly creation and we see men and women coming to a proper adulthood, happy at last to belong to God and be subject to God. When God is everything to everyone, humanity will be restored in love and goodness and wisdom. Those who suggest that there may be misery or envy at an ordering of eternal life which includes both punishment and reward, fail to see that when God is everything to everyone we will at last love justice and goodness and mercy and wisdom and righteousness. We will love his ordering of things because we will love him, and we will not envy in the slightest those whose reward is different or greater.

Other images of the future

My method has been to describe our future in terms of the future of Jesus Christ. Once we have established this procedure, we are free to observe the richness of the rest of the Bible's language about 'heaven', or, as it may be better to call it, the triumph of God. It is at this point that we can usefully observe that it is called 'home', for example, as though we are wandering here, far from safety, and our going into the next age is our 'going home'. We are exiles, and heaven is our promised land, our land of rest, from which we will never wish to be permanently separated. Or, we may use the language of 'reward', where God is willing to meet us and reward us for what we are in Christ. Or, we may think of the riches of eternal life, life that is abundant, as John calls it. Or, we may remember the tremendous celebration of our security in God's victory in some passages. Or, we may think of the sheer weight of glory, or the pleasure of a feast, or the marvel of a wedding, or the security, culture, companionship and riches of a great and perfect city.

I have already noted that the Bible continues, necessarily from our point of view, to use the language of time for eternal life. It is worth noting, too, that all language is strained by this subject and that it is no accident that the book of the Revelation to John contains the most sustained use of imagery in the Bible. In describing the beginning and the end, the Bible's language becomes increasingly pictorial. This does not mean that we should thereby lose confidence in it, but should recognize that we are now, more than ever, speaking of things beyond our comprehension, where the usual resource of describing things unknown by things we know begins to fail us. Language about God in general has this problem, of course, but the difficulty is greater at the beginning and end of things. We do not despair of our knowledge, however, remembering that faithful Israelites, nurtured on the Old Testament promises and prophecies, recognized Christ when he came, even though they could never have guessed the details of his life and death beforehand.

Aspects of God's triumph

What is the reality of God's triumph as we study biblical imagery, and especially that of the new Jerusalem at the end of John's Revelation? We see here that God's future, God's consummation, has four features. Firstly, God's consummation creates a *community*. The very point of the holy city, the new Jerusalem, is that the dwelling of God is with men and women, that his people, his church, are gathered together. Unlike the cities of human construction, in God's future true community occurs. When God speaks about humankind it is never in the abstract, in isolation, but humanity in relationship, in fellowship, in community. This is our destiny.

Secondly, God's consummation rests on *righteousness*. There is no doubt in Scripture that evil is hateful and needs to be defeated and banished if we are to be happy. In this city there will be no wickedness and no wicked persons. Admission is granted only to those who have been cleansed and who now love the Lord their God with all their heart and their neighbour as themselves.

We will be transformed into the people we ought to be: we will rejoice in goodness and justice.

Thirdly, God's consummation brings *peace*, not the peace of apathy and neutrality, but the well-being of those who love and are loved. There will be no more suffering, for 'God will wipe away every tear from their eyes, and death shall be no more . . .' (Rev. 21:4). The tree of life from Eden reappears at this point in Revelation, with leaves 'for the healing of the nations'. The overwhelming sense of the city is one of a glory and perfection which will infinitely satisfy. The idea of a static perfection that leads to boredom is fatuous; the God who made this extraordinary world in which we now live, is hardly likely to create a dull and uneventful future environment. Our passion to be entertained by tragedy, by conflict, by evil, by risk, arises from our fallenness. I hardly think that a population prepared to be entertained by television can as yet judge what will truly enthral and satisfy the human spirit.

Fourthly, God's consummation is centred on *God*. There is no sense here of God being at the centre of adoring masses, for ever wrapped in smug self-contemplation, aided by the flattering praises uttered by sycophants. He is indeed praised and worshipped, but our praise of him is evoked by his infinitely tender and gracious care of us. 'Behold, the dwelling of God is with men,' writes John in the Revelation; 'he will wipe away every tear'; 'To the thirsty I will give water without price from the fountain of the water of life'; 'I will be his God, he shall be my son'; 'they shall see his face, and his name shall be on their foreheads' (Rev. 21:3–4, 6–7; 22:4). No temple is needed any longer, since their access to God is immediate; no light is needed, since he is their glory. Our communion with God is the communion of those who love and are loved.

In the cities of the earth we have, as well as security and companionship, the works of our hands from which we draw satisfaction. Our communion with God in heaven does not exclude this at all. As long as we realize that the centre is God and the Lamb, we can see, too, that the nations walk in the light of the city, and the kings of the earth bring their glory into it. The gates, John says, are never shut and 'they shall bring into it the glory and the honour of the nations' (Rev. 21:26). The power of God never excludes the labours of human beings. Indeed, his final word on the triumph of God concerns the work of the servants of God: 'and they shall reign for ever and ever'. Thus the dominion God gave Adam and Eve is restored and the work of our hands will be revived and restored to us.

In short, the Revelation of John has given us one biblical picture of the End; the End which is also an extraordinary new beginning. I would not like to suggest, even though it is in the Bible, that it is more than a glimmer of what God has prepared for those who love him.

The triumph of love

There is, however, another description which is worth sharing, as well. For the Bible at one point contrasts our present and our future, by saying that we are now like children, immature in speech, in thought, in reasoning, in knowledge. The moment will come, however, when we give up childish ways and become adult. In the present, says the Bible, 'I know in part; then I shall understand fully, even as I have been fully understood' (1 Cor. 13:12). But lest we think this means abstract rational thought, Scripture concludes, 'So faith, hope, love abide, these three; but the greatest of these is love' (1 Cor. 13:13). Our 'full understanding' is not an access to the secrets of running the universe, but is our knowledge of God, our relationship with him. He has an immeasurable, undeserved love for us, and we will reciprocate, not with the love which is a fixation that enfeebles us, but with that adult love which bears all things, believes all things, hopes all things, endures all things; the love that cheerfully serves. Whatever else we discover in the End which God has planned, it will include this: that at the very heart of the universe there is love.

To discuss or think about

1 What three stages will mark the coming of the End?
2 Contrast the common images of our destiny (or heaven) with the biblical picture.
3 What are four characteristics of the consummation of God's triumph?
4 In what sense will we 'understand fully' (1 Cor. 13:12)?

Conclusion to part 1

I began this part by thinking of Sydney as typical of a great city which provides the security, the culture, the commerce and the companionship that the human spirit needs. And yet I began, as you may remember, referring to a perfect summer day, but feeling that there was more. For our cities display our sins, they mock our aspirations and, even when they are at their best, we are reminded of our imperfect experiences of love and fulfilment. At home, even in the best of homes, we are not at home.

And so we turned for our beginning to the End; the goal where God's purposes for us are to be fulfilled. There is still so much that we do not know; we 'see in a mirror dimly'. And yet, we can see by focusing on what the Bible says about Jesus Christ, the essence of the future consummation. We can see that God purposes the fulfilment of our humanity in a way that will profoundly satisfy our better, truer hopes as well as his own plans for us and the world.

I have argued, too, that the bold step of starting at the End is justified because of the light this throws on the present and our responsibilities in the present. Far from making us passive or lethargic citizens of the present age, the Christian hope is a key agent for change, for perseverance in the right, and for understanding of the nature of humanity. These things will, I trust, become clearer in part 2 which is entitled 'Who rules the world?', and is a study of God and humanity in that grotesque conflict that the human race has undertaken to wage against its Creator.

PART TWO

Who rules the world?

In one of his memorable Professor Challenger stories, Sir Arthur Conan Doyle portrays his hero, a brilliant but eccentric scientist, acting on the belief that 'the world upon which we live is itself a living organism, endowed, as I believe, with a circulation, a respiration, and a nervous system of its own'. How would you act upon such a belief? The man of science has no doubts. He intends to penetrate the hard outer crust and harpoon the sensitive inner part.

As the story opens, a shaft has gone down eight miles and the engineers have uncovered a sort of living, breathing, bubbling jelly, rising and falling in slow palpitation. The moment of truth arrives. The Professor has arranged for the substance to be pierced by a steel borer, and the press, the scientific community and a vast crowd have gathered. Those down inside the shaft saw that 'the exposed surface was like a boiling pot': there were 'great grey bubbles', 'agitated activity', 'a dark purple fluid', 'a heavy smell' and 'the throb of life'. Then, finally, the 'iron dart shot into the nerve ganglion of old Mother Earth and the great moment had arrived'.

I cannot, of course, tell you all that happened next, but the thing which I think is especially unforgettable is the noise: 'the most horrible yell that ever was heard'. 'It lasted a full minute, could be heard in France, and was unequalled in history ... It was a howl in which pain, anger, menace, and the outraged majesty of Nature all blended into one hideous shriek.' The inimitable Professor Challenger became 'the first man of all men whom Mother Earth had been compelled to recognise'. The name of the story? *When the World Screamed.*[1]

Callous though we are as a race, the thought of plunging a monstrous dentist's drill into the very earth itself (or, perhaps, herself?) is shocking. Professor Challenger, however, admirably represents the breezy certainty of an earlier age. He justifies his action on the ground that it will increase scientific knowledge. For him, twentieth-century Anglo-Saxon man is the master, the ruler of the world.

Today we cringe at such chauvinism. Challenger's crass attempt to dominate nature is bad enough. But his kind and his era represent tyranny in human relationships as well – man over woman, white over non-white, rich over poor. Today we cry out against the injustice and oppression inherent in sexism and racism. What gives any of us the right to control or dominate? What gives us authority over others? Can even legitimate authority be exercised without corruption? Who rules the world?

In part 1 I described the purposes of God for us – how they will come to pass in the End, and how, with the coming of Jesus Christ, they are being fulfilled even now. We saw that God's new age had begun while the old one continued. We began to understand that God is a God of purpose and of promise.

We can now better interpret the time in which we live and the factors that shape it. In studying the purposes of God, we can see what relationship has been set up between God, the world and the human race. In particular, we can see more clearly who God is, and who we are and what is his programme for us in this world and the next.

In part 2, therefore, I am going first to discuss the question of 'Human tyranny', then give a closer look at the real state of humankind in the subsection 'The once and fallen king'. Thirdly, and chiefly, we will study God and his relationship with creation under the heading of 'The true King' and, finally, I will propose a 'Joint rule' for this earth.

CHAPTER 3

Human tyranny

Human dominance in nature

We gladly call the lion 'the king of the beasts', but we know that we are not numbered among his subjects. Indeed, we are the rulers of the beasts, no matter what they think. We name them, we classify them, we herd them, we breed them, we slaughter them, we eat them, we tame them, we save them, we trap them, we destroy them. We consult with no other species on how to run the planet; we do not even consult them about issues that affect their lives. It is true that some resist our incursions, and with some we carry on a war, or at best live in a truce, most notably with the insects. But even cockroaches may be poisoned, and we certainly never ask a sheep for permission to move it to a different paddock. If one culture worships the cow, another culture eats her, making her a strange god after all. There are some marvellously gifted animals, but we have no rival as the world's dominant species, the ruler of creation. Indeed, we distinguish ourselves from all else by speaking of 'Nature', meaning creation apart from us.

Human culture arises from our dominance as we turn the earth's resources into the world we want. We speak, we count, we read, we classify, we measure, we explore, we map, we build, we plant, we destroy, we hunt, we fight, we use tools and advance to machines, we create alloys and plastic, we heal, we co-operate, we specialize, we sing, we play, we paint. If the world threatens us or mystifies us we reciprocate with our cultural devices, our religion or our technology, for example, to tame the world of nature and make it do our will. In doing so, we seem to enhance human wisdom and power.

Contemporary protest

There is articulate protest, however, about the assumption of species dominance. In part, at least, this protest is directed specifically at the contribution of Christian teaching to the problems of our world. Ironically, what was once regarded as a point for pride is now thought of with shame. It was once thought to be a wonderful vindication of Christianity in general and Protestantism in particular that the Industrial Revolution and the rise of capitalism occurred in protestant England. It was all part of the dominion over the earth that was the charter of mankind according to the Bible. Now, however, we have come to see the rapacious and exploitative side of all this: that progress has been very costly; that the oceans and the atmosphere are suffering; and that the very command to 'be fruitful and multiply' needs to be reversed if we are to give the earth a population it can sustain. Christianity stands directly accused of contributing to that species pride which is endangering the whole earth.

The protest against species dominance is wider than that, however. I will isolate three forms. Firstly, there is the protest against the obsolete attitudes behind much of our thinking about humanity and nature. We are accused here of persisting with ideas equivalent to belief in a flat earth or that the world is at the centre of the universe. We know that, physically, this is not true. Now we need a new Copernican revolution to force us to see that our species is not at the centre of things either – whether of the universe or of the world. Our anthropocentricity is both wrong and dangerous. It is the crime of speciesism, the preference for our own kind above others for no valid reason. We must now concern ourselves with animal rights, for example, and, more important, we must recognize that evolution does not owe us a living. If we fail the earth, it will replace us with another dominant species, with complete impartiality. We will be like the dinosaurs.

Secondly, there is the protest against intellectual flabbiness. Physics, in describing nature, has now revealed the sheer vastness of space, the longevity of time and the connection between them. As well, the randomness of our existence as individuals and as a race has become apparent. It is myopic to persist in thinking that put beside all this, we as individuals, or we as a race even of five billion, have any real significance in the scheme of things. It is only in the unrelenting realization of our own trivial importance that we can have a true estimate of ourselves at all. Talk of ruling the world is mischievous nonsense.

Thirdly, there is the protest against moral delinquency. The old sins have passed away, but new ones have arisen to take their place. The world of nature is fundamentally 'balanced' apart from human interference. It is in a state of harmonious equilibrium and, left alone, it will rule itself in a sort of organic democracy. If we would abandon our pernicious attempt to exercise dominion over nature and, instead, harmonize, letting nature run things, we would be happier and more humble. It is interesting to note the religious aspect of this and especially to see how, as the dominant-human model decreases in importance, nature becomes personified, as though someone must rule. Sometimes 'Nature' is deified rather than personified, and our harmony with her becomes worship.

The spirit of power

I have illustrated my point with reference to our attitude to nature. My point is even clearer, however, when we consider human relationships. Here we can see a spirit of power at work in which we try to control, manipulate and use each other. Attitudes of superiority and discrimination are rife. We can see such attitudes channelled through the social institutions approved by Christianity. We see the domestic tyranny of the male, for example, or the oppression of the poor by business, or the heartless rule of government. We have such bitter experiences of injustice through discrimination that the whole exercise of any authority at all, even parental authority, has become problematic.

Once again, we do not lack social critics who see evils such as class injustice, racism and sexism as endorsed by Christianity. Once again, it is said that our obsolete attitudes, intellectual flabbiness and moral delinquency are all too apparent. Once again, there is much point in what is being said, if only because we are all infected with the spirit of power, with the conviction that the ruler of the world is me; that is to say, the individual who either has or longs for the power to order existence to suit himself or herself and control others.

The purpose of human life

Quite clearly, therefore, there exists a sharp critique of much conventional human thought and practice in connection with human relationships and the natural world. Great questions are posed here both for Christianity and for human culture in general. A central question is this: 'What is the purpose of human life? Why are we here?'

To some, of course, this is not a real question. There is no purpose; individuals must make of life what they will. Others, though, are prepared to suggest a purpose or goal for human existence even though there may be no God to give purpose. The hedonist, for example, sees the chief end of life as pleasure or happiness. The utilitarian will emphasize the greatest happiness of the greatest number. The libertarian will emphasize the absolute value of human freedom, so that any act or lifestyle is permissible as long as it does not compromise the freedom of another person or actually harm them. The Marxist, the feminist, the conservationist may well all have their own version of the purpose of human existence.

So, too, does the Bible. Already I have given some explanation of the End or purposes of God in the first part. We turn now to the Christian teaching about the human race not merely as what comes next in a list of topics, but where the Bible places it – in the context of God's purposes for the world. What do these purposes show us about the human race and the problem of human tyranny?

The once and fallen king

True authority

We cannot evade the complaint levelled at Christians that we believe humankind is accorded a unique and dominant place in God's order of creation. 'So God created man in his own image, in the image of God he created them ... and God said to them, "Be fruitful and multiply, and fill the earth and subdue it"' (Gn. 1:27–28).

The geocentric, anthropocentric view of things is written large in the Bible. Adam names the animals and is given permission to eat of every tree but one in the Garden of Eden. Animal skins clothe Adam and Eve, and the ground is cursed because of them. Furthermore, from the very beginning, human authority in the lives of other human beings is endorsed, especially in family and public affairs. There is a structure of authority, responsibility, obedience and submission.

The chief modifying feature of this authority is that it is given, not inherent. It is on loan, so to speak, from God. The responsibility we hold is on trust, and the trustee is accountable. Human authority is never thought of as absolute – it is derived from God and is exercised under God.

More needs to be said, however, about both the uniqueness and the authority of human beings. While our unique significance remains, our capacity to rule has been, according to the Bible, seriously flawed.

The significance of humankind

The prior insight that humankind is significant to God arises from the first part of this book about the End or destiny of the race. We saw the Bible's view that the End finds us in Christ, with Christ and like Christ, in submission to God. We conclude from this that we are both helpless and precious to God. We are helpless to save ourselves. History on its own cannot create heaven; our cities will never match the new Jerusalem, but the fact that there is to be a new Jerusalem and that God has populated it with the nations shows that he regards us as precious. So, too, does the humanity of Jesus Christ – that the Son of God became man in the first place and that he is willing to act as the pattern for the race in the age to come shows that the Bible speaks the truth when it says that God loves the world.

We note also that the life of our race in history is highly significant and meaningful. God's future judgment of the world with its meticulous sifting of human lives, words and thoughts is, of course, awesome to contemplate, but it tells us this as nothing else can: we matter to God and everything we do and say and think matters. Current convictions that human life is meaningless, that there are too many of us and life is therefore cheap, that you can live either well or badly without it mattering at all, are totally wrong. The doctrine of the resurrection of the dead and the judgment to come asserts the continuity of the person beyond this age and the significance of this age for what lies beyond. Contrary to the views of some critics, however, such convictions do not provoke social and political quietism and passivity. They strengthen those who see the need for improvement because they know that their work done in Christ's name is not in vain. It is part of God's own work which he will use and reward.

We also note that the fulfilment of humankind is to be found in the triumph of love and justice, in community with others. The picture of heaven that we have shows us that we will be just and love justice, that we will draw satisfaction from loving and being loved, that we will be in relationship with others whom we may serve. Especially, however, we will be glad to live under the dominion of God himself, and in that order of things we will exercise the rule that he has given us. In short, our special place is reaffirmed, but it is humanity transformed into Christ's image and now ruled by God.

Our knowledge of humanity's future, or rather End, gives us an anthropology which contrasts with those of our contemporaries. For example, in the Christian view, any anthropology based on the idea that death is the end of existence is bound to be defective. We must dissent, too, however, from those who push our race from the centre of God's purposes in the name of chance or evolution or the size and complexity of the universe, or the concept that nature is alive and can rule herself. Nor can we be accepting of an ethical view such as libertarianism which has no passion for love, for justice, or for community, preferring a tolerant individualism. Nor is it possible to accept the validity of materialist views in which we work out human fulfilment by human effort within history. Humanity and its individual members are so significant that God will not let them go – whether in justice or in mercy, he shows his love.

Humanity's flawed rule

Not only is our race uniquely significant, however. Its capacity to rule is seriously flawed. The Bible reveals that God has committed authority over the world and even authority over others into our hands. The exercise of this authority is intended to be under God's authority, and in accordance with God's way. We were never intended to be independent.

We readily agree, therefore, that the complaints of the environmentalist about the way that the world is abused are true; so, too, the unfavourable verdict of the Marxists, with their talk of alienation and oppression, and class against class; so, too, the analysis of feminism with its revelation of the immorality of male power; so, too, the observations of the libertarians with their points about intolerance. Indeed, simply at the level of literature, the Bible itself is one of the world's greatest exposures of human folly, crime, corruption and greed.

It is interesting that, with the one exception of Jesus himself, none of the biblical heroes is perfect. Moses and David committed murder, and David added adultery. Saul's reign was a disaster. Solomon led his people astray. Daniel confessed his sin. Abraham, Peter and Paul all failed. Furthermore, when God set up his own, his special people, and put them in the Promised Land with a full and clear exposition of his law and with human agents to teach it, their national history was a disgrace (although no more a disgrace than our own). When intentions, hopes and ideals were so high, the consequences in broken promises, idolatry, greed and oppression were appalling. It is as though some terrible irrationality had entered into their national existence which meant that they behaved like a drunk, confident that he could walk a straight line while stumbling about out of control. The prophet Jeremiah concluded: 'The heart is deceitful above all things and desperately corrupt; who can understand it?' (Je. 17:9). The history of the church (including what we can see in the New Testament) has been no better.

Modern psychology has transformed our understanding of the personality and has outdated much of the language that Christians have traditionally used. In the popular mind, psychology has so explained human motivation, especially by concentrating on the experiences of growing up, that questions of right and wrong, of guilt and innocence, are inappropriate or outmoded. But the study of psychology does not pretend to start with a morally committed view of the human person. It explains where it can, but it does not judge. In particular, it does not profess to bring the judgment of God to bear on human behaviour. That, I would say, is the function of the Bible, which is concerned to give us the proper assessment of human experience. It is an assessment which foreshadows the ultimate critique of the day of judgment.

When the Bible analyses human life from its point of view, it gives the habitual experience of moral failure the ominous name of 'sin'. As we have seen from the prophet Jeremiah, it locates the problem as one that is lodged at the core of the personality, in the heart as we would say. In the place where the ordinary person finds that motive, emotion, will and reason are entwined, there he or she also finds an irresponsible and irrational tendency to sin, affecting all. It does not make us wholly bad, but it can make even our best efforts tainted. It is not under control, as though by an act of the will we can bid it stop troubling us, for it has affected the will, too, and it arouses unbidden thoughts and desires which design ill on others. It shames us and attracts us at the same time, since we cannot imagine ourselves as different and we do not want to change.

The measure of failure

I have called moral failure 'sin'. Its reality is measured by the demands of God on human life. It is easy enough to deceive ourselves about the nature of our sinfulness by adopting our own standards or the standards of our community to measure it by. But the Creator has retained the right to set the standard, and his law is holy, good and just. Even more significant than the law, however, is the life of Jesus Christ, the one true and faithful human, who kept the law. If we wish to know the truth it is useless to employ a lesser measure. You cannot adequately explore a wrecked building at night with a small torch; you need the sun. In the light of the sun you will discover that, even if your sin may be less outwardly obvious, less outrageous than other people's, it is real and the difference between you and them is ultimately insignificant.

The measure of God's law reveals two further things not popular to the human mind. The first is that sin is not merely individual, it is corporate. Corporate in the sense that all are victims of its malign influence, but corporate, too, in that we aid and abet each other in sin. We look to each other for guidance, we tempt each other, we cheat each other and so teach each other to sin. Our children are born into households in which sin is manifested in ways subtle and crass. And yet our children do not need to learn from us. It is a struggle to teach them manners, let alone goodness. It seems, and indeed the Bible confirms, that the race as a whole, and all the members that are born into it, are disposed to sin. We love it. We hate ourselves for it. We are gripped by it. We are accountable for it.

The Bible traces this back to a moment on the very edge of human history when Adam and Eve, under the influence of the serpent, chose to disobey God and have thus transmitted sin to the human beings associated with them. Whether this is a strictly historical account or only the pictorial account of an historical event, the Bible's analysis of our present experience is undeniable: we simply and habitually assume all others to be like us, sinful.

The second thing that God's law reveals is that our chief sins are not against our fellow humans but against God himself. Most people reduce the Ten Commandments to the last four or five. God begins by seeking the whole love, with heart, soul, strength and mind, of all people for himself. The human race owes God its grateful thanks; instead it is perpetually creating lesser gods, including people themselves, to worship. The first sin was rebellion against God's rightful authority. It continues, especially in our present age, in the form of pride or the determination to be free of God and God's interference and ownership. That is why the most respectable person may be judged, in the end, to be the most desperate and corrupt sinner. Even his 'goodness' may be an act of rebellion against God. Who rules the world? If the choice is between God and us we know at once what to do. We rule him out.

It is not surprising, then, that feminists, Marxists, environmentalists and others are right: we rule the world very badly indeed, taking on more authority than we have, abusing our authority, exalting ourselves above others, polluting the world. We are like children let loose in a sweet shop. Nor is the amount of pain and suffering in the world and caused by the world surprising. The Bible's brusque verdict is 'In Adam, all die' (1 Cor. 15:22), and the world is not how God created it – the home of a sinless race. The Bible says that it reflects our sinfulness in being a place of suffering, and it suffers with us, for sin taints everything. It has not become evil in itself, but it is the sort of world for guilty sinners to live in. It may be that were we not sinful some of its mystery and danger would be transformed by our untarnished perceptions and we would not suffer as we do. That is now not the case, however. In a final indignity on the creation, we take parts of it – animals, trees, money – and worship them rather than God.

The Bible does not 'explain' what we call the problem of evil – a good and powerful God, an innocent life, an experience of agony – but it insists that our thinking should include the factors of the spread and effect of human wickedness, the presence of divine justice in this life and beyond, and the final determination of God to create a new heaven and a new earth in which dwells righteousness. Indeed, it reveals also, although with little detail, that we have not sinned on our own; that human sinfulness is part of a far deeper spiritual wickedness in the cosmos, and that human redemption involves God in a wider conflict about which we remain largely ignorant. After all, the title 'ruler of this world' is not given to humankind in the Bible, but rather to the Evil One, Satan himself.

In sum, what does Christianity regard as the purpose of human life, 'the chief end of man'? Contrary to the modern mood of 'putting man in his place' as an insignificant, recent species occupying a small planet on the edge of the universe, Christianity affirms the central significance of our race. If you go to 'the heart of the universe', to God himself, for his perspective rather than that of the earthbound physicist, our size and frailty become irrelevant. To him we are precious, though flawed. To reject this view leads to the nature worship of some modern conservation movements, to naturalistic ethics, and to pessimism. We need to be committed to the significance of individuals and our race, but we also need to recognize that we are a fallen people on a journey to God's End, and we need to challenge just as sharply as the conservationists, feminists, Marxists and other modern moralists the abuses of power in human life.

To understand the implications of this we turn in the next chapter to the very heart of the universe, to think about God himself, who is the true and lawful King of this world.

To discuss or think about

1 Humankind has assumed dominance over the rest of nature. Why does this now arouse protest?
2 To what extent are the protesters right in tracing this dominance to the influence of Christianity?
3 How does the Bible account for the disastrous way in which we have exercised our dominance?

CHAPTER 4

The true King

The character of God

In one of the most famous encounters of the Bible, God meets Moses at the burning bush and reveals to Moses his name: 'I AM WHO I AM', or 'I will be who I will be' (Ex. 3:14). A person's name was, and still is, regarded as his reputation, his character. It tells us something vital about the person. The Lord's name, as given to Moses, is a promise that, as we see and hear of his words and deeds in the rest of the Bible, we will discover who and what he is. I have chosen three sets of words to describe him – independent and committed, glorious and gracious, ruler and servant.

Independent and committed

The Bible portrays God as King, as Sovereign Lord. There is only one God and he has no rivals. As the Creator he is prior to all things in time; he is free from the limitations imposed on us bodily creatures by space and time, being able to exert his power anywhere or everywhere for however long he chooses. We need never fear that we will go beyond his power to see, to know, to protect, to judge. Nothing in all the world can force itself upon him or make him act in a way that he does not choose. He is unchangeable, but he is not unchanging. He cannot be frustrated or delayed, by nature, history, human or spiritual forces, but it is proper to speak of him grieving, loving, waiting, being angry, even suffering.

Such a God is awesome and may thus be thought of as utterly distant from us in every way. Not for a moment, however, does the Bible allow us to see him as anything other than involved. His sovereignty is thoroughly committed to sustaining and ordering the universe he has created. We must not think that the independence I have described is arbitrary, depending on God's mere whim from moment to moment. It is founded on his settled and committed character, his consistent disposition to truthfulness and to faithfulness. He is a truth-speaking, promise-keeping God. His independence is never the freedom to lie or to retract his commitment. We have seen, furthermore, that this commitment is entirely purposive – the universe has an end, a goal, a meaning, and the Lord God is committed to bring it to pass.

Glorious and gracious

The Bible warns us that God is not like man, and the glory of the Lord is a constant reminder that this is so. Glory is a word which, in a sense, epitomizes the vision of the invisible God, full of that brightness, splendour and dazzling light which overwhelms us and casts us down. It is also the 'weight' or majesty of his presence. But the Bible is speaking here of more than visual display. It is referring to God's holiness, his otherness, his separateness. He is separate from us in power and might, of course, but the Bible also and chiefly refers to his quite dazzling goodness, his wisdom, his righteousness. Confronted with this we would collapse in moral confusion and shame as Isaiah did (Is. 6:5). God's righteousness not only separates, it consumes, for no unclean or unjust person may stand in his presence and, as the Bible says, 'our God is a consuming fire' (Heb. 12:29).

And yet, the glory of God is seen in the face of Jesus Christ (2 Cor. 4:6). It is his righteousness which goes out by Jesus Christ full of grace and mercy, to forgive, to cleanse, to declare righteous, to redeem, to save. For this God is a saving God. Further, his salvation is extended first and foremost to his enemies, to those who vociferously dispute his right to rule the world, to be its king. God is never more glorious than when he graciously saves. If his name reveals the truth about him, it never does it better than when we discover it to be Jesus Christ.

Ruler and servant

It is already clear that God is sovereign in his freedom from all external restraint. We need to notice, too, that he has especially the dominion over this earth; that he is its true and rightful Lord and he alone. Such authority, according to the Bible, ought to receive the unquestioning obedience of those over whom it is exercised. We must note as well, however, that the authority of God is a serving authority, that it is an authority exercised for the good of the other – God is love. God's authority is not tyrannical and self-centred, but responsible and caring. It is real authority for all that, but authority of a particular sort; authority, but not unfettered and unfounded authoritarianism.

God in himself – one, and three in one

I have mentioned that the name of God reveals something of his character. But there is a second reason why the Bible chooses such language to talk about God. In giving someone your name, you are, in a sense, giving them yourself. You are identifying who you are, you are inviting relationship, you are giving access to yourself. Thus when God reveals his name, it is an act of self-giving, not merely cosmic intellectual enlightenment as some may suppose. We humans have named everything else in the universe, but God names himself.

In relating to us as the Master who serves, God does

not lie or deceive. What he shows us of himself is true of his inner being. God is not only loving towards us; he is, and always was and always will be, love – love in himself, love at the heart of the universe. In a miracle of his mercy, he reveals further something of what this means as we encounter God the Father, God the Son Jesus Christ, and God the Holy Spirit – the one God who is three in one.

In Jesus Christ and the Holy Spirit we encounter those who come from the Father. They fully share his divine nature and prerogatives. They are not created beings. They do not compromise God's unity, yet they are distinct from the Father and each other. There is complete equality of standing in this threefoldness of God, and a permanence, but there is also distinction and order, the Father sending his Son into the world, and the Spirit being sent by Father and Son. Here we see in the being of God that ruling service which we see in his relationship with the world itself.

The astonishing revelation that God is three in one emerges in the Bible in different ways. It is shown in the way that God saved the people of Israel from their enemies on numerous occasions by endowing various human saviours, like judges and kings, with his Spirit for his work. Ultimately, he endows Jesus, his only Son, for the work of saving the world. It is shown in what God says, for the intimate linking of Father, Son and Holy Spirit is a notable New Testament pattern in various places. By contrast, men, and even angels, are carefully distinguished from God. It is shown in what we find God to be towards us: loving, saving and applying salvation, as we shall see later.

Nor is it that the Father could be God apart from the Son, for who the Father is can be understood only from a knowledge of the Son. The Son defines the Father; the Father defines the Son. Each of the three depends upon and works fully with the other, equal and yet ordered, showing us what love is and showing why it is that God does not need the world or anything outside himself. Before the world was made, God was alone, but he was never solitary.

Is it best to take at least a partial step in response to the feminist challenge and refer to the Holy Spirit as 'she'? We ought at once to assert that God is neither man nor woman, male nor female. But the step of calling the Spirit 'she' in order to endorse the rights of women would distort the doctrine of the Trinity. Far too much emphasis would then fall on the difference between the ones that have revealed themselves to us and we would have three gods not one; or, at best, a divine family of Father, Mother and Son.

It is also fatal to give up personal pronouns in speech about God in order to avoid calling God 'he', for it excises his personhood and makes him a distant object. To go the whole way and call God 'she' and 'Mother' is to deny his right to reveal his own name in his own terms. The Word of God became flesh as man and to use the feminine pronouns of God is to set up unbearable tensions for God's revelation of himself. Admittedly, we are told that in heaven there is neither marriage nor giving in marriage, and we may be sure that it is our weakness which stops us from seeing the possibilities of being human, let alone of being God. But for now we must be content with what is given. What we see, in fact, is that the fulfilment of love, which is the goal of human life, can be found in the very person of God himself.

The world and God

Dependent but distinct
Given that this is the nature of God, what can we say of the world (and by extension, the cosmos) over which he is King and Lord? We can see, of course, that it utterly depends upon him for its creation and its continued

existence. There have been those who have thought of the world as eternal rather than created at a point in time, or with time. I must admit that I find this view hard to square with the Bible in which God created all things. Others have wanted to consign God to the realm of the first cause alone and thus banish him from the daily workings of the world. Even more clearly this is at odds with the Bible which, if it can be applied directly to a scientific account of things, would be better heard to say that God works all things at every moment and that such 'laws' as we observe are his regular ways of behaving. Nonetheless, and this point must be made just as clearly, God works through and with the entities he has created and, in one sense, we do not need him as an explanation for what is occurring around us. Energy is all of him *and* all of nature; we lift our hands by his power working with and in our own.

God is committed to the world and it depends upon him, but it is separate from him. He is not to be identified with the world. Idolatry is the taking of a part of the world and identifying it with God. This is as false as the error of pantheism which identifies the whole world, including us, as God. Pantheism achieves a sort of ultimate inflation of honours, a pseudo-aristocracy of the spiritual world. Both pantheism and idolatry involve the worship of the creature rather than the Creator.

Human rule and the scientific approach

Over the years there have been religions and philosophies which have endued the world with spirit. In such cases, spirit either penetrates so that matter is the form by which we assimilate spirit or, alternatively, spirit affects matter from without so that objects, buildings, stars, charms, water, and circumstances can tell for us or against us and we live in a world of fortune, of luck. In this case, we must find the objects and/or prayers which will influence the spirits and persuade them to be on our side at the crucial moments to give us 'luck'.

The truth that God is one, the supreme Lord, the Maker of heaven and earth, and that all things depend upon him while being separate from him constitutes a revolution for this way of thinking. At the heart of the universe is love and order. The world is literally disenchanted. One good and utterly reliable spirit rules the world and it moves entirely at his behest. There is order and consistency; there is purpose and there is goodness, for the world has been created good and we have been given permission to use it, with thanksgiving, for our good and with no bad conscience. The old spirits are banished. The world is cleansed of their influence. God's steady and wise providence, in which all things work together so that we may be like Christ, replaces luck and fortune. The stars are merely the servants of God; the superstitious use of holy objects, lucky charms, blessed water, lapses. The division of human experience between this spirit and that spirit, this saint and that saint, disappears. The way is open for us to study the world on its own terms and for its own sake, believing that it is, in principle, comprehensible. The way is open to resume our rule of the world.

Of course, it is not as simple as all that. The belief in the one God sustaining but separate from the world encourages a scientific approach to reality. It is just as possible, however, for an atheist to adopt the same approach, relying on what he or she may call the axiom of the regularity of nature. Christians will glorify God as they work, thanking him for the marvels of this good creation. The atheist will use the same method but will fail to glorify God, and may even put the mechanism by which God has created all things (assuming it to be an evolutionary creation) in the place of God. This confusion of categories seems to satisfy the vague religious feelings of some, for here is a 'god' as uncaring and impersonal as anyone can wish for. Whether God has created the world in a way that can be described by evolution I cannot say.

It is only necessarily inconsistent with the Bible if the process is accorded the status of God.

More important, however, is the limitation on the human exploration of reality which we must observe. The progress of human understanding has been accompanied by error, defeat, superstition, opposition, persecution and stagnation. There can be no doubt of the stunning and wonderful results achieved in the last three centuries (for which we should thank God), but there remain knotty problems, apparently insoluble difficulties, profound disagreements, uncertainties about the philosophy of science itself, not to mention the human costs of the results. We may say that the world is, in principle, comprehensible, but that is a statement of faith and there are mysteries enough to make it a very bold one. The world the scientist studies sometimes reminds him or her of the possibility of a god of some sort; sometimes it only confronts him or her with apparent chaos.

Furthermore, and this is a feature of the last two decades, the very standing of the scientific enterprise has come under cultural threat. Scientists inflated their own importance and science has suffered an inevitable but painful decline in prestige. This has been accompanied by an appropriate growth in philosophical modesty as the special place of the observer in scientific method has been recognized and the relativistic nature of results made clear. At the same time, however, issues concerning the moral consequences of scientific work have been raised: not so much the morality of doing science at all, but the morality of the use of science in weapons, in wasteful luxuries, in the use of animals for experiment, in the potential interference with human life. Furthermore, certain well-publicized cases have demonstrated that the personal integrity of the scientist as a researcher and communicator cannot remain unquestioned in all cases. Can an immoral person be a good scientist? The question sounds absurd, but it deserves attention if this is, in fact,

God's world. We must not accept 'the scientist' as a benign, wise and powerful abstraction, ever again. He or she is a sinner like us and one who fights against God's rule, as we can see from the results.

Acknowledging the rule of God, then, enables us to view the world appropriately and begin to take responsibility for it under his dominion. But it is perfectly clear, once again, that even our best efforts remain flawed. That is the truth about human nature and its inherent sinfulness. Nonetheless our sinfulness is no argument for being passive. Christians have something to say in our present crisis about humanity's relationship with the world. We have a challenge to the way we live here and now. We have a vision appropriate for our times – the possibility that even now we may share God's rule. It is to this subject of joint rule that we now turn in chapter 5.

To discuss or think about

1 By contrast with humankind's flawed domination in the world, what does God's name tell us about his true kingship?
2 How does the revelation of God as one yet three cast more light on the nature of his authority?
3 Why is it important to view God as separate from the world he sustains?

CHAPTER 5

Joint rule

Some societies approximate to the new Jerusalem more than others; some eras demonstrate a concern for justice and truth and love. It is perfectly clear, however, that no human effort – physical, mental, spiritual or moral – can create the new age, the heavenly city. Having plotted where we are in world history, we can see something of what the End will be, but we know that our best efforts will fall short. Nonetheless, such conditions of our dominion as work and marriage are in place, and the imperative to exercise our rule remains. Human culture, using the term broadly, is the result of this authority.

'Culture' indicates the improvement of nature, and especially human nature, through education and intellectual development. Our work in the world develops us and develops the world: humans become builders; rivers become dams; trees become furniture; grunts become language; the air carries music. Here is the nub of the problem, however. It is precisely this development of the world which causes most alarm to those who are critical of the dominance of our species. Our culture expresses our self-centredness as a race, our determination to rule the world in our own favour without respect for the law of God. Furthermore, much of the blame for this state of affairs is laid on the Christian faith with its endorsement of human domination. It is western culture which has most bruisingly confronted both the world itself and the delicate human patterns of life.

The malaise of our culture

We are raising here the question of the quality of our culture and specifically our western 'Christian' culture. By quality, I mean chiefly its moral and spiritual quality, but there should be no distinction between moral quality and effectiveness in the broader sense. If I am right, Christianity will want to say that persons will make better scientists if they are good rather than bad (of course this is simplistic, but I think that the point is valid). I want to argue, in fact, that our culture is suffering from a long-term illness (I can't think of a better word) and that it has to do, not with the presence of Christian values, but the absence of them – reflecting, of course, the truth that the age to come in its final form is still beyond us.

Take the institutions which provide stability and order in our society, which act as the voices for many ordinary people, or as the channels through which they receive support and nourishment: churches, schools, universities, hospitals, unions, the home itself. Is the effectiveness of any one of these not under question, under threat, under doubt? Or consider the professions which, since their development over one hundred and fifty years ago, have provided local leadership, trusted advice, specialist care, quality service: doctors, teachers, clergy, lawyers, social workers, engineers, economists. They were once synonymous with integrity and skill. Consider the vital work that is done by those who disseminate information: journalists and other media people. Without them our western democracies could not possibly survive; with the ones we have, we do not know how we will survive. Think of the yawning chasm that exists between what musicians, novelists, poets and artists want to do and what a community, whose tastes have admittedly been coarsened by TV and not repaired by education, are prepared to hear and see. We could go on and on. We could consider architecture and ugliness; politicians and expediency; commerce and exploitation. We could talk about sport and greed. We could discuss the use of obscenity in public and private speech and the fate of the language. We could think about the rightness of sustained economic growth as a goal for society. We could think of our obligations to the poor of the earth.

I refuse to concede that the picture is all gloom, or, on the other hand, that our loss of confidence is all wrong. I am trying to point to the extent of a malaise in culture, however, a malaise that many times over has exacerbated the natural cynicism of our character so that we no longer believe in the good intentions of others, especially the leadership. We do not believe in authority of any sort. There is developing a loss of nerve, a sort of individualism in which I will make my own choices notwithstanding any obligations others may suppose me to have. I am self-determining, for I trust no-one. I will not be a co-operative member of a team without being paid well to do so. I will assume that persons I have to deal with are incompetent, tyrannical or greedy until proven otherwise.

For myself, I am most deeply concerned about the state of the family and the home, starting as it ought with one man and one woman in loving and exclusive union, whatever its subsequent individual history may be. Here, it seems to me, is by far the best place for persons to be loved and to learn what love is, to become loving and not cynical. Here we can be given the support that makes us strong, stable, healthy and well-balanced individuals. Here we learn what it is to be men and to be women, for better or for worse. It is true, and obviously true, that families can often be unhealthy and even hellish. A society which fails to cultivate the family, however, and which endorses especially individualism, promise-breaking, sexual infidelity and selfish assertiveness, is a society which has become culturally suicidal. The purveyors of the libertarian vision that human obligation is fulfilled merely by not damaging your neighbour should have the agony of the last generation and the present one on their consciences.

Renewing human culture

Can a culture be renewed, regenerated, cleansed? Given that in a sinful world a perfect human culture is impossible, can we find a clue to ruling the world in a way which approximates to the intention of God? Not, I judge, by retaining any respect for libertarianism, which has no culture but the culture of the self. Not, I think, by the personification or divinization of Nature, as though we can achieve wholeness by the worship of the world. Nor should we be tempted for a moment by the vision of a monolithic Christian culture in which every human endeavour from astronomy to zoo-keeping will have its place and receive detailed instructions on how to proceed. The Bible no more tells us how to be a doctor or plumber or clerk or pianist than it gives us the secret of penicillin. God intended that we should have dominion, and the Bible, by being silent, grants us freedom to develop our culture within the basic principles he has given us.

We would need to have, instead, a recognition of the right authority of God. We would need to have a willingness to be responsible ourselves under God, that is, to have authority. We would need to exercise this authority in God's way. We would need to share a common view of humankind and its value and destiny. Our anthropology would need to acknowledge the reality of human sin and hence guilt and accountability (not merely in criminal matters) and the reality of forgiveness. We would need to admit the preciousness of the life and the significance of the words, deeds and thoughts of every individual of whatever age and social importance, including the preciousness of unborn life. We would need to recognize our corporateness; that we belong to one another and should aim to build the other person up through love.

At the heart of this we must deal with the tension inherent in human culture, a tension between cultural activity aimed at power and cultural activity aimed at service. If you think through the list of institutions, professions, activities and leaders that I mentioned you will see the significance of the question. Where culture exists for personal satisfaction alone, or for control over others, or for the acquisition of wealth, or for the establishment of personal security, it merits all the criticism heaped upon it by social observers: Marxist, feminist, Christian. The Christian faith insists on an opposite motivation, however. The work of our hands and our minds must be for others, first to please God, second to bless the neighbour, third to be responsible for the world in which we live. Our responsibility is global, and it extends both to nature and especially to the men and women of our race wherever they may be found.

In this we should reflect God himself, who rules through serving and serves by ruling. There is nothing wrong with authority and leadership in any sphere of life, from home, business, the armed forces, politics. It becomes perverted, however, when authority is not understood as the responsibility to *serve* by leadership. Our community leaders and institutions have provoked a crisis by not convincing us that they are operating in the public service. Our business, commercial and professional lives show little concern for public service. That abstraction of the accountants, economic man, has been inflated and imagined to be a real person, with catastrophic results, since economic man is not moral man and knows nothing of neighbourliness, let alone love. A. J. P. Taylor notes that one good thing bequeathed to India by the British was a Civil Service that was actually motivated to serve, and he links this with Christianity. 'Corruption fell out of fashion,' he writes. 'Public service took its place.[1] If media persons, lawyers, doctors, shop owners and assistants, clergy and counsellors asked themselves: 'Who is this I am dealing with? Is it not a precious human being, made in God's image, with a future beyond this age?'; if they asked, 'How am I to behave? Is it not in serving love?' we may begin to achieve cultural regeneration. If they asked, 'How can I serve God in this task, however mundane?' we may begin to see something of how God intends that we should rule his creation as his agents.

To my mind, it is easier to see how such an approach will touch our educational institutions than how it will shape the work of the novelist or artist. The idea of a self-consciously 'Christian' novel or painting is pathetic. There are novels written by Christians, but surely no Christian novels as such. We need to discuss creativity and aesthetics with this in mind: how does this activity stem from love? How does it reflect the creativity of the God who rules by service?

In speaking of the renewal of our culture through loving service, I have dwelt almost exclusively on human relationships rather than the environmental questions I emphasized at the beginning. For this I make no apology, for the Bible so assesses the significance of things human as to make our chief responsibility fall there. That is not to ignore our relationship with the world, however. In this world we have been placed as guardians or stewards under God, and with his loving service as our pattern. That we may use the world's resources for human benefit is one thing. That we should voraciously exploit them without thought for their replenishment or for our real needs is another. If the Christian ethos has contributed to ecological disaster, it is the usual distortion and corruption of what is good by human sinfulness. Human science reflects humanity's grandeur and brutishness as does all our culture. We ought not to personify or divinize nature – that is a way to disaster – but we should be its trustees and stewards, recognizing that its real ruler is God and that apart from us it will not reach its appointed End.

To discuss or think about

1 What is at the root of our culture's malaise? How does it manifest itself?
2 How can our culture be renewed?
3 In the particular sphere to which God has called you, what implications might the idea of 'ruling by service' have?

Conclusion to part 2

Join rulers with God? God's servants in ruling the world? We do not need the environmentalists or the feminists to tell us how far short of any such ideal we fall. The ideal mocks us; sin is our plague. We are frustrated at our lack of progress, and even when a particular culture demonstrates the loving service of which I spoke, it is a temporary and inadequate phenomenon.

Our basic problem is not with others or with nature, but with God. He rules the world, but we believe that we should do it without him. Jesus joined issue with this pattern of thought when he came proclaiming that 'the time is fulfilled, and the kingdom of God is at hand' (Mk. 1:15). For God not only continues to rule the world, he also speaks. The fact that he speaks and what he says will be the subject of part 3.

PART THREE

Is God dumb?

Hardy's god

The great English author, Thomas Hardy, once referred to 'the dreaming, dark, dumb Thing that turns the handle of this idle Show'.[1] Whatever Hardy's own religious views were, and I am not for a moment claiming to speak about them, the words are a brilliant description of the god who, to the minds of many of our contemporaries, is at the heart of the universe. For the sake of this discussion, I will call it Hardy's god. Consider the implications.

This god is without relationships. It is a thing, deliberately stripped of the personhood which makes fellowship, communion and love possible. It is dreaming; abstracted, therefore, from the world of men, high above us, on a different plane altogether. It is dark; obscure to us, and perhaps itself, inhabiting a world of shadow and gloom.

This god is without speech. It is 'the dreaming, dark, dumb Thing . . .' Of course, this is another facet of absence of relationships, for speech is the richest, most subtle, most enduring vehicle of human relationship that we have. To be dumb or deaf is, even more than blindness, an affliction which cuts you off from others.

This god is without purpose. It 'turns the handle of this idle Show'. Hardy allows his god power, the power to make history jangle along, but it has no more interest or purpose than is displayed in the idle turning of the handle of a mechanical device which makes puppet figures go through their trivial and preordained motions. History exists, but in the hands of such a god it is, indeed, like life to Macbeth, 'a tale told by an idiot, full of sound and fury, signifying nothing'.

This is real atheism, not the sort of bold illogic which simply declares that there is no God without ever being in a position to know. Here is the atheism that allows there to be a god, but a god who is a dreaming, dark, dumb Thing; a god whose only power, if power it be, is to make us jog through our paces in a meaningless ritual.

Nothing could be more unlike the God which the Bible portrays. That God whom the atheists reject is alleged by the Bible to be alive and active; he is the servant-ruler described in the last chapter who sustains and orders both history and creation with a dynamic, purposeful energy and a burning love. He is not dumb, but is a speaking God, who claims to have the right to rule us now and in the future.

In fact, of course, I have been assuming all along that God spoke. In the first part, when I described God's End, his goal, his purposes, I was able to do so only because of God's promises. Promises are words. They are words which secure the future for us. They are words that call for faith and hope. When we began with the End, we were really saying that God has spoken.

The aim of this section is to investigate the speech of God, what God has said and is still saying. This is called the doctrine of revelation and is usually treated first as a sort of entrance hall to all doctrine. It is intended to answer the question of where the knowledge of God may be found, before going on to expound that knowledge.

The unfortunate effect of this procedure, however, is that the function of God's revelation, and hence its nature and authority, is obscured. The chief purpose of God's revelation is not to fill in the gaps in our knowledge. It is to restore his rule over us, his kingdom; a rule that we have been disputing and contradicting. God's word is integral to his kingdom and must be seen in the context of his purposes. It is for that reason that we turn to his revealing and ruling word at this point in the exposition of Christian doctrine.

Competing visions

In chapters 7 and 8 I am going to concentrate on God's word. In the first place, I will describe Jesus Christ as the Word of God; secondly, I will relate Jesus to the covenant word of God which established and ruled the nation of Israel into which Jesus was born. Before we turn to these sections, however, more will be said in defence of Hardy's god. The idea that God does not speak is based on some genuine insights and problems, and they need to receive attention.

I do not think that we are dealing here with issues that can be investigated simply on a set of agreed, objective principles which will then lead logically either to the virtual atheism of Hardy's god, or to the Bible's theism. Admittedly, there are issues of fact and there is the necessary use of reason, but we have here what can be described as competing visions of what lies at the heart of the universe; of different, very different, angles of approach. As we decide between them we are being asked to use our intellect, but more, our judgment based on our experience of life as to what is true and what is false, what is right and what is wrong. I am not saying that it is merely subjective and relative, but that the issues are more like those involved with getting married than deciding whether a piece of arithmetic is right or wrong.

I am not intending, therefore, to discuss the pros and cons of each point of view in the light of reason. There is an important place for such discussions, but my task is different. It is to describe the Bible's 'angle of approach', its 'vision of the universe', so that you can be helped to enjoy it if it is your own, or even adopt it as your own. Nonetheless, however, there are various things to be said in defence of Hardy's god, and, strangely, they are things which will help us see the Bible's God with greater clarity.

CHAPTER 6

The god of Thomas Hardy

I have already observed that Hardy's god is popular in our society. Most people want to retain the word 'god' if only so that they may blaspheme. The oath is still administered (although there is the alternative of affirmation) in our courts of law. There is also the comfort of knowing that, in an emergency, God is there to be spoken to and, like luck, may well be favourably disposed from time to time. 'Are you going to put your faith in God's hands, or look to some more secure means?' as I once heard a radio journalist ask someone caught in a cyclone.

God the obscure

There can be little doubt, however, that the idea of God is obscure. The capacity of his power is unclear; the extent of his interest in individuals is unknown; the concept of obedience to God has become redundant; his righteousness and wrath have become distasteful; his word has become incredible. There is a folk-memory of the Christian God, but it is a god shorn of the very things which made him personal, which made personal relationship possible. Some would now also say that he should be robbed of his traditional gender and we are to speak of him in such a way as to make clear that he is not simply masculine – but then how are we to speak?

The difficulty of speech about God

The problem that we are experiencing with the traditional God corresponds to a crisis concerning all human language. In Christianity, and especially in Protestantism, words have occupied a central role in knowing God. Human language, from the Bible in the first place, but also in lessons, sermons, lectures and books, has been the chief, even exclusive, vehicle of communion with God. Language as a vehicle of human relationships, however, is threatened at both a popular and a reflective level.

It seems that in everyday life, for example, bitter experience has taught us to be cynical about promises and their capacity to hold us on course. Our cynicism is illustrated by our capacity to ignore our marriage vows, and it is not surprising, perhaps, that many people no longer want to make them. We have been cheated too often. There is no need even to illustrate the wicked perversion of language in public arenas of speech, such as the media, political life and advertising. Our speech often becomes the vehicle for self-aggrandizement, as in the horrible language of abuse and cursing that is so common. It is not surprising that we prefer to receive the news in pictures, nor that human relationships have become both more transient and more sensual, and that we find it hard to relate to a God who comes to us via the word.

The problem of language also confronts those academic disciplines (and their professional counterparts) for whom the written word has traditionally been of central importance. The interpretation of texts in literature, in law, in history and in theology has become more uncertain. Should a text be divorced from its author or approached through the known predilections and experiences of the author? Indeed, does any text have only one authorized meaning? Can language be trusted to convey it? Can texts transcend their culture? These and many other problems assail the disciplines. And the matter is not merely theoretical. Consider the effect of different methods of approach to the interpretation of a document such as a country's constitution. Should it be what the authors intended, what the words say, or what the authors would now say in different circumstances?

Theology has its own special problems in this area and they, too, contribute to the general uncertainty about God. In part, the problems have always been recognized. If God is not man, indeed is not created, but is of a totally different order of existence, how can we speak of him? When we communicate at a human level there is common ground; even in talking to someone of a different language, we have bodily existence in common. If God is unlimited spirit, without body, how can we communicate? Is it best to concentrate on saying what he is not, in the hope that this will lead us to what he is? Would it be better simply to admit that we only ever speak of him by most imperfect analogy? Could you start with, say, a human – made in God's image – and then affirm that God is the supremely eminent example of virtues we see in ourselves, such as power, wisdom and love?

The difficulty of finding God

The breakdown of language has contributed, then, to God's obscurity in our culture. We will not trust this medium of communication; God has become remote and impersonal. In this situation, little help has been received from either rational reflection or religious experience.

Human exploration
The older apologetic of rational reflection, which relied on our capacity to prove the existence, and, to some extent, the nature of God, has not been a success. The rational proofs of God's existence, it is now believed, are far from decisive. In any case, they hardly lead to fellowship with

God. When, as happens from time to time, physicists speak of 'God' in connection with their research, it carries little weight, given the constantly changing nature of physics and the sort of God that is allegedly discovered.

Religious experience seems, at first, a more promising avenue of knowledge. There are various intimations, hints, evidences of God in the world which at least offer the hope that we can discover what he is like by following such clues. There is the nature of the world, which suggests design; there is the experience of conscience and mortality, which suggests a higher righteousness and future judgment; there is a variety of experiences such as answer to prayer and the sensation of being guided by a higher power; there is the phenomenon of the well-nigh universal religiousness of the human race.

And yet, even when we are prepared to take such experiences seriously, they lead little further, on their own, than to Hardy's god. Mircea Eliade observes, 'Neither the religions called "primitive" nor those claimed as polytheistic are ignorant of the idea of God who is the Creator, omniscient and all powerful. Yet we have only to look at things a little more closely to realise that such supreme deities enjoy hardly any actual religious worship ... the highest heavenly Being has declined in practical religious importance; he has withdrawn from human beings.'[1] He could be talking about our own religious situation, where attention is fixed on the power available to the religious person rather than the remote and abstract God preached in the churches.

Indeed, it is interesting to see in the churches themselves something of the triumph of Hardy's god. Modern theology has abandoned a religion in which the word of God is identified with the Bible. The result is that there is every evidence of an unfulfilled longing for personal intimacy with the divine, for reassurance, for close guidance, for spiritual power. We see a heightened interest in the sacramental mysteries, in worship as personal communion with the Holy, in a hunger for miracles, in the sanctity of the archaic, whether buildings or liturgy. The burning problem is the attempt to achieve intimacy with the remote God.

In short, there is little enough in the world, in human reason or in religious experience to lead us beyond Hardy's god.

The Bible's verdict

With this rather gloomy conclusion, the Bible agrees. It is fully conscious of the weakness of human language, as the story of the Tower of Babel reveals (Gn. 11:1–9). It is fully conscious, likewise, of the manifold religious aspirations and experiences of humankind. Indeed, human religiosity in the Bible is generally the evidence of a good thing gone wrong. The Bible sees humankind as having some flashes of understanding. We see the truth that this is God's world, that we owe everything to him, and that there is such a thing as accountability for right and wrong. It immediately asserts that this knowledge is suppressed, however, and demonstrates itself only in false religion and imperfect righteousness. Our religion, like all the rest of human culture from language to art, is affected by our great quarrel with the true God.

Thus the Bible asserts that the human attempt to find God is futile, because he is not the sort of God we wish to find. In Scripture it is the idol who is dumb; God is always the speaking God (see Is. 41:21–34; 46:7). If we cannot have access to a power that can be manipulated ('My will be done'), we would prefer a dumb, dark Thing, a non-relational far-away god, to be approached on our terms and worshipped as we see fit. We know enough to condemn us, but not enough to move us. We may long for intimacy, but not at any price. We no longer possess the will to know the truth.

The Bible's view, therefore, is not that language has ceased to be a valid vehicle of communion between God and man, but that humans prefer a dumb god. The Bible has confidence in language. It believes in the word of God and sees it as the instrument by which God saves and rules his people. The Bible believes not that we can find God, but that he has found us. It claims to contain a revelation that has invaded our world and that will enable us to trust in language again. It brings us the God who speaks.

The revelation that has invaded the world comes to us in a twofold form, both parts of which may be called God's word. In the first place, there is Jesus Christ. Secondly, however, there are the words by which he comes to us; words which were addressed to Israel, before they were addressed to us all as our written scripture, the Bible. The chapters that follow discuss the twofold word, Jesus Christ and the Bible.

To discuss or think about

1 What ideas about God are prevalent in our society?
2 What factors in our society surround the idea of language about God with difficulty?
3 Why do rational reflection and religious experience fail to lead us 'beyond Hardy's god'?

CHAPTER 7

The God who speaks

The nature of God's word

The powerful word

As I have indicated, the Bible itself shows no embarrassment at the idea of a God who speaks. It also describes prophetic ambassadors who speak for God and who ensure that God's words are written down, remembered, consulted, believed and obeyed. Every reader of the Bible is struck with the grand opening sequence which outlines the creation of the universe in stages. God is not portrayed as bringing creation to pass through battle, through sexual union or through manufacture from raw materials. Rather, we hear of him bringing all things from nothing by his word of command, thus demonstrating an effortless, ordered might. In this way, the author exalts the power and skill of God without confusing him with creation itself. His word is personal, intimate and yet distinct from creation.

The power of God's word is celebrated elsewhere in the Bible. Since he is a God who cannot lie, his word of promise is absolutely secure. When God says that something will be, it happens inevitably. His law is as perfect as he is. Indeed, the word of the Lord, in whatever form we find it – sustaining the universe, making wise the simple, ordering the unruly lives of his people, rebuking and admonishing, making promises – has the same impact as the Lord himself. To obey his word is to obey him; to trust his word is to trust him; to repudiate his word is to repudiate him. You cannot strip him of his word and have him remain as he was. That is the agony of modern theology.

The relational word

It is no accident, therefore, that the word of God should be so prominent in the first chapters of the Bible. In fact, in this respect we should compare the opening of the Bible with another great occasion, the opening of Jesus' ministry, in which he came preaching the word (Mk. 1:14–15).

When men and women were created, they owed their very existence to the word of God: 'Then God said, "Let us make man in our image, after our likeness; and let them have dominion ..."' (Gn. 1:26). More, he also, by his word, laid down the pattern of their future lives, telling them to 'Be fruitful and multiply ...' (Gn. 1:28), but also imposing limits upon them: ' ... of the tree of the knowledge of good and evil you shall not eat, for in the day that you eat of it you shall die' (Gn. 2:17). This constitution was to be their charter for living. They only had to consult their memory of God's word to know the purpose of their lives and the limit to the freedom he had given them. He ruled them by his word.

That word of God was, of course, broken. The assault on the integrity of Adam and Eve came in the form of an attack on the word of God. The serpent of Genesis 3 cast doubt upon the word from the beginning, and the actual disaster was a mutiny against the rule of God in his word. In language used later in the Bible, they repudiated the kingdom of God, with results that are obvious to this day.

Jesus Christ and God's word

It is exactly this issue that Jesus addressed as his ministry began. He announced the imminent arrival of the kingdom of God, and called for repentance and faith in his word, the gospel. It was not, of course, that God had ceased to rule the world in the interim, but that the moment had arrived when the people of God should again surrender to his rule and his rule be perfectly restored. What we ought to note at this point is the part played once more by the word of God. The work that Jesus did was preaching the word; that which they should believe and obey was the gospel word. They were to submit again to God's rule through his word.

There was a monumental difference between Jesus and the other prophets of the Bible, however. Not only did Jesus bring a message from God; he himself was the chief content of the message he brought. He announced the kingdom and he revealed that he was its King. The prophets pointed to Christ; he accepted their witness. He was in himself the light of the world, the bread of life, the giver of living water, the perfect revelation of God, unsurpassed and unsurpassable. 'He who has seen me,' said Jesus to his astonished disciples, 'has seen the Father' (Jn. 14:9). Not surprisingly, when these disciples began to preach after the death and resurrection of Jesus, their message was summarized as: 'Jesus Christ is Lord.' This was not opposed to the kingdom of God. This was the kingdom of God.

The identity of Jesus Christ

Such a development poses a strange and terrible question for any serious reader of the Bible, namely the identity of Jesus Christ. An impossibility has been suggested. If there is one thing abundantly obvious from the Old Testament, it is the truth that there is only one God. The ultimate King of God's kingdom is God himself. The possibility that Jesus Christ is the King forces us to enquire who he is and what he is. It becomes the question on which the whole of Christianity pivots. Your answer will finally determine whether you regard Christianity as a tragic mistake, a cruel hoax, or the very key to life and the whole creation. To put it starkly, in terms of what the Old Testament seems to say – indeed, in terms of common sense – it is not possible that the man from Nazareth, child of Joseph and Mary, should be the Lord. Alternatively, it is not possible that the Lord God, ruler of the universe, should somehow constrict himself into the space and life of a genuine human being. It seems that if you are going to say that Jesus Christ is Lord, it is only because you think that he was man masquerading as God or God masquerading as man.

This dilemma arises, however, from inadequate concepts about what it is to be human and what it is to be divine. Consider what true humanity and true divinity reveal about this problem.

True humanity

The Bible expands our assumptions about both humankind and God. Very naturally we imagine that we understand completely what it is to be human. We do have some understanding, but it is an understanding from a rebellious point of view. We are corrupt versions, smudged copies of the truth. Christ is the perfect man, perfect in righteousness; he is the true image of God. He is what we will be, and he shows some of the possibilities for being human. I am not for a moment suggesting that he was of a new and different order. On the contrary, the Bible calls him 'the last Adam', and shows that he lived among us, was tempted as we are, and experienced death. When we think about whether the Lord God has become a genuine human being, however, we must remember that it was this human being that he became.

True divinity

Consider, too, our assumptions about the one God. The fact of there being one God is true, taught painfully to the human race over many years. As we saw in chapter 4, however, the very book which does more than any other to establish God's uniqueness then reveals that in this uniqueness there is a threefoldness, a tri-unity. It cannot be accounted for by saying that there are three gods, or, at the other extreme, three names for the one god.

To our surprise, therefore, we find that within the life of God there exist from all eternity, relationships. For there is one who addresses another, and one who delights to hear and respond, and a third through whom both are at work; and yet all three are one in being, purpose, will, wisdom, might and standing. The experience of relationship which, for us, can only be extrinsic, is with God intrinsic. In God's mercy, furthermore, he has revealed the names by which we ourselves may know him and address him. He is Father, Son and Holy Spirit; not names given merely for our benefit, but names that are eternally true and reveal the relationships that exist in God's life. For it is clear that the Father is not the Son and neither Father nor Son is the Spirit.

We ought not to be so surprised as we are. After all, we ought to have realized that God's life is different from our own. I suspect, however, that, whereas we can imagine him easily like some gigantic and complicated piece of machinery, we are less comfortable with the idea that his personhood is so extraordinarily far from our own. We resent the depths and possibilities of it. We resent not being able to imagine what it is like to be God. Hence our most sophisticated idolatry (or image-making) is to insist that there is only one God but to deny the true God who is one in three and three in one, and whose relational personhood is profound beyond our imaginings.

It is the one God of philosophical monotheism who is incapable of involvement with the world. The Bible however, reveals an astonishing, an unlooked-for development in the story of God's relationship with the world. We think, from our human-centred vision of the world, that after God created the world it somehow got out of hand and required an emergency measure. It was more or less luck, therefore, that God is triune, making an entry into the world somehow possible. In fact, of course, the triune God created a world, and the triune God created a race where such a thing may happen. For the Son of God to enter the world as God and man has never constituted a problem for him, however little we may understand it. It is how he planned it to be.

The image and Word of God

The question that I have been addressing is that of the identity of Jesus Christ and the problem of whether we are forced to think of him as God masquerading as man, or man masquerading as God. I have been arguing that the force of this dilemma arises from our inadequate assumptions about both God and man. I want to turn now, however, to see what it is that the Bible says about Jesus Christ and what is, in fact, claimed on his behalf. In order to do so, I am going to use as starting points two of the many descriptions and titles given to him: the image of God, and the Word of God.

The image of God
Firstly, Paul calls Jesus 'the image of the invisible God' (Col. 1:15). It was, of course, man (male and female) who was created in the image and likeness of God, according to the first chapter in the Bible: 'Let us make man in our image, after our likeness; and let them have dominion . . .' (Gn. 1:26). Their likeness to God was especially reflected in the rule they were to exercise over the earth. They revealed God as they ruled. Their rebellion against God corrupted their capacity to reveal God.

When Jesus Christ is called 'the image of the invisible God', therefore, there is a deliberate contrast with Adam after his fall into sin. Jesus Christ reveals the truth about

God. Unlike Adam, he stands for the true, the genuine. God is invisible, and the sheer fact of his invisibility makes his presence problematic for humankind, and creates difficulties in speaking about him, since language depends on commonalities. The 'knowledge-gap' between God and us has been bridged in Jesus, however, and we may know what God is like because of what Jesus says and does. God is not so distant that we cannot see him in Jesus who 'reflects the glory of God and bears the very stamp of his nature' (Heb. 1:3).

Of course, the Son of God has always reflected the glory of God from all eternity, but his becoming human did not prevent or hinder his role of revealing God, it enhanced it. He is the image of God not only before his coming, but in his life, and especially in his death. Indeed his death on the cross is the most telling revelation of who God is. For Jesus Christ to be the image of the invisible God for our benefit, he had to be authentic man. His manhood does not obscure his deity; it enables him to reach out to us, and say, 'He who sees me sees him who sent me' (Jn. 12:45; cf. Col. 1:18, 20).

Thus, as well as specifically calling him 'a man', the New Testament shows that he was born, he ate, he grew, his life was endangered, his parents lost him, he displayed ignorance and asked questions, he loved, he wept, he prayed, he rejoiced, he was tempted, he was betrayed, he was crucified. Included in the full range of human experiences was limitation – limitation of time, history, culture, gender. We feel that such an entry into the world by God himself is impossible only if we fail to recognize the nature of God's glory; that he is never more glorious than when he is love, when he rules by serving. For, ultimately, Jesus Christ is never more clearly the image of the invisible God, he never more clearly shows what God is truly like, and yet he is never more human – weak and vulnerable – than when he dies on the cross. Here is the servant in glory. Here we see, insofar as it is possible for mere humans to see, that Jesus Christ is both true God and true man.

The Word of God

Secondly, John calls Jesus 'the Word of God' (Jn. 1:1–18). We have already seen how, according to the Bible, God creates and rules all things by his powerful word. Now John identified the Word of God as a person, and reveals that he is the ruling principle of the universe, since 'all things were made through him, and without him was not anything made that was made' (Jn. 1:3).

We see at once that salvation through Christ is not some last-minute plan of God to redress a human mistake. Christ is not an emergency measure; he is the pattern, power and purpose of creation. God's whole work of creation and redemption is bound together in Christ. Elsewhere the Bible reveals that the universe was made through Christ, is sustained by Christ and is intended for Christ. As we saw in the first chapter, Christ is the goal, the End of all things.

As with 'image' so, here, the Word is clearly chosen to emphasize the revelation of God, that the void created by sin and language difficulties is bridged from God's side by his revelation. Furthermore, the Word is not said to be *like* God, he is said to be with God and to be God. He is said to be light; the true light that enlightens all. The revealing power of the Word does not stop with the inspiration of prophets like Moses, however. To God's great glory, 'The Word became flesh and dwelt among us, full of grace and truth' (Jn. 1:14).

The sheer daring of this is breathtaking, for God becomes human and at once becomes vulnerable to the hatred and rejection of a race that is long accustomed to be his enemy. It does not mean, of course, that God was diminished in some way, as though the Word ceased to be the Word, for how, then, would he have remained truly God? It does not mean that he chose to inhabit an existing human being, raising him to a new degree of divinity, for then how would this be dwelling among us? He became flesh, but he did not change into flesh. He became flesh; he did not simply inhabit flesh. The difference between God and humankind makes this awesome; the likeness makes it possible.

Human minds have never been able to penetrate the paradox involved. The Bible is saying that the Word of God has come into the world; that we know him to be none other than Jesus Christ; that he was and is and always will be the Word, God himself; and that he was and is and always will be human. Not some new hybrid, unlike God and unlike man, a mixture; not God pretending to be human or a human pretending to be God; but the one person who is now both God and human, and who, therefore, is God's great Word to us. For it is in him, as he is in the Bible, as the Word made flesh, that we see both the grace and truth of God and what it is to be human. This Word is the fitting Lord of our race.

The god of Hardy's phrase, 'the dreaming, dark, dumb Thing', is the sort of god we can arrive at with unaided human perceptions. But the God of the Bible is not dumb. He has a Word, a mighty Word, which finally has invaded the world. The truth has become a person, God's great speech to us, his great moment of self-revelation and self-giving, his service to a disobedient race, the focus of our renewed obedience. This astonishing insider is the substance of the gospel and the Bible, the essence of the Christian story.

If you are looking for a 'way in' to the Christian faith, to assess its truth, here it is. It is in the study of Jesus Christ, the Word of God. Yet note that this Word comes to us in words. His entry to the world does not bypass human language, or human culture and history. It could not, for then it would fail to be a genuine entry. If you wish to find Jesus Christ and assess him it must be under the conditions which he himself submitted to, namely in the context of his own people, in their words about him and in his words to them. The Word of God comes to us clothed in words and, if that is true, the Christian gospel has the power to cleanse and rejuvenate human language.

Thus our treatment of the doctrine of revelation comes now to the words in which God reveals himself. We find these words 'at work', so to speak, creating, moulding, ruling, challenging and sustaining God's people. As we study this aspect of revelation, therefore, we are beginning to gather something of the nature of the church, too, for the words of God are its foundation. Likewise, what we say about these words will have a bearing on our convictions about language itself.

We turn, therefore, to our final major subject of this section, to Israel, the people among whom the Christ was born. It is here that we find the words of God that promised him and the words of God that describe and convey him to us.

To discuss or think about

1 What distinguishes the 'speaking God' of the Bible from 'Hardy's god'?
2 In what way was Jesus himself 'the chief content of the message he brought'?
3 What dilemma arises from the statement 'Jesus is Lord'? How does the doctrine of Jesus' humanity and divinity help us to resolve it?
4 The Bible presents Jesus Christ as the image of God and the Word of God. How do these descriptions shed more light on his humanity and divinity?

CHAPTER 8

The God who makes promises

There are two highly important areas in which to assess Christ which I will leave to part 4, namely his life and his resurrection. In one sense, however, prior to these and, in another sense, resting upon them, is the whole question of his relationship to his own people and their history. For when he presented himself to them and claimed a continuity with their history, a God-given continuity, most of them decisively rejected him. And so to this day there are those whose Bible finishes at the end of what we call the Old Testament, and there are others who are convinced that the message of Jesus, the New Testament, must be added if it is to reach its proper conclusion.

This is not a trivial issue. What we are dealing with here is a God-given history and a God-inspired book. If the Old Testament does point to Jesus Christ, then so does God himself. But I am not proposing to make the assessment as such, only to describe the foundations of the culture that we are talking about and go on to draw out the implications if Jesus Christ is regarded as their fulfilment.

It is somewhat strange, of course, to be talking about the fulfilment of a nation's history, even if one accepts the gigantic importance of some individuals within it. Great individuals change history in music, literature, politics and war. You can also set out more fully the antecedents which help explain them while also showing how independent they are. But something more is at stake in the present case, namely the fulfilment of history.

Israel – the covenant nation

A nation founded on words of promise

Israel traced her history back to certain individuals from a select family, the family of Abraham, who lived about two thousand years before Jesus. The Jews believed that, on the whole, they were the genetic descendants of Abraham. This descent would have had little value, however, if it were not for Abraham's special history. Since God chose Abraham, God had entered into a unique relationship with him, a relationship marked by solemn promises on God's part and faith on the part of Abraham. In essence, the promises were that Abraham would have many descendants forming a great nation, that they would possess the land of Canaan, that they would be protected and blessed by God and that, through them, the families of the earth would be blessed (see Gn. 12:1–3; 15:1–16, *etc.*).

From the form which these promises took, a solemn oath accompanied by memorial signs, the arrangement was known as a 'covenant' or 'testament'. God's covenant was his gift to his people, as we can see by the stress on 'promise' contained within it.

We should note at once that this covenant and the ones that flowed from it and expanded it were the constitutional documents of Israel. They were not forgotten or lost. There was national apostasy but also the constant acknowledgment that they were to live and die by these words. The words created and moulded the people; they were given, not invented. It is as well to note the form of the constitution, namely promise. The words reflect the God who is a God of purpose, who has an End in view. Promises are always forward-looking. They are capable of fulfilment, even of fulfilment on more than one occasion. Furthermore, the chief way of receiving promises is by faith – you believe and so act as one who trusts. Words beget faith.

These promises met with various fulfilments. There was, indeed, a nation, even an empire; there were extraordinary military successes; there were failures too, as other promises of God concerning judgment came true; there were blessings for the Gideonites and curses for the Egyptians; there was prosperity and blessing, at least for the Queen of Sheba and other foreigners, if not yet for all the families of the earth.

A nation governed by the covenantal words

As well, there was the expansion of the covenant by other covenants, not inimical to the first but extensions of it. Of these, the covenant at Mount Sinai and the covenant with King David are the most notable. From the covenants there came the various institutions that governed the life of the people of God in this stage of national existence. Central to that existence was the precious gift of the law of God, which set up the institutions and provided authoritative guidance for an ancient rural people, surrounded by paganism, living under God's rule in the land promised to them by God. The law kept them separate from the nations around them. It insisted on a purified, non-image centred worship; it created a sacrificial system and a priesthood; it ordained the valid places of worship; it arranged the annual calendar. As well, it gave the 'case law' by which one could interpret prohibitions against theft, murder, adultery, Sabbath-breaking and lying that were at the heart of the law. It also encouraged the spirit of love and neighbourliness and justice which befitted God's people in their communal life. So, too, did the wisdom writings and the psalms which were created to aid the people living under God's rule in the Promised Land.

Three further features of the life of Israel, as revealed in the Old Testament, require special mention. The first was its history. The people began as a covenant nation, held in covenant by God's promises and responding with faith which led to obedience. Their story became a record of failure which, in accordance with the provisions of the covenant, merited, and often received, the punishment of military oppression. Their woe often turned to repentance, and the Lord in his mercy, without any obligation on his part, provided saviours who released them from bondage. The greatest act of salvation was the release from Egypt, and the greatest saviour and prophet was Moses. This exodus provided the pattern and the language for the others, and was commemorated in speech, song, prayer and feast from then onwards, even to the present day. Thus there was set up a great tension between the glowing promises of God and the dismal experience of God's people; a tension quite familiar to the contemporaries of Jesus who were oppressed by Rome. From this tension came the hopes of a national Saviour who would introduce the kingdom of God.

Second, there was the explanation of her history. The description I have given does not arise from some modern historian's interpretation of Israel's story. The nation's history was interpreted by God's own Spirit and written down and preached about by the prophets. Even the chief historical books of Israel were regarded as 'prophetic' in this sense. Other prophets, men like Isaiah, Jeremiah, Amos and Malachi, observed the contemporary situation, compared it with their knowledge of the covenants and made remarks both critical and predictive. The prophets, like the Wisdom Literature, formed an authorized commentary on the Law, which itself accompanied the covenantal provisions.

Third, as must already be apparent, in choosing Abraham, in entering into covenant with him, in keeping faith with the promises, in adding the Law and sending the prophets, in revealing his name to his people, in creating institutions for worship, the Lord was setting up his kingdom that had been repudiated by Adam. The covenant, which is, of course, verbal, is the instrument of

God's rule, and its nature as promise is a token of his intentions to restore all things in accordance with his purposes. The covenant describes and secures God's 'End'.

The Bible – a covenant book

Promise and fulfilment

It is essential to note, therefore, that when Jesus appeared, he was not a lonely religious genius who was thrown up more or less accidentally by history. The Jews already believed that the Lord God had made them his people, and that their laws and their institutions were of divine origin. They were already people of a book and that book was the Bible. From a Christian point of view their Bible was inspired though incomplete. But God had prepared them to relate to him through the sacred words – the Law, the Prophets and the Writings as they were sometimes called (although some used only the Law). That was not all of their religion, but it was basic to their religion. And it was the promise or covenantal nature of the Bible, together with the fact that their history had not so far fulfilled the expectations of God's coming kingdom, that led to the possibility that an individual may be the awaited, the hoped-for Messiah.

Jesus came not merely to announce the kingdom, but as its King; not merely as one of the prophets, but as the Messiah; not merely as a national saviour, but as the Son of God; not merely to fulfil the word, but as the Word. This posed for his contemporaries a series of tremendous questions, including what sort of kingdom and what sort of messiah was before them. He was crucified as a royal pretender, but not all Israel rejected Jesus. Many accepted his claims and believed, especially after testimony to his resurrection was preached. It was on this solid ground that Jesus required them to judge him. He believed completely in the inspiration and truth of God's word, as did his foes.

The only question was whether he fulfilled it. For Jesus, these books were of God, inspired by God's Holy Spirit, and therefore true. Whatever such books promised must come to pass because the promises were God's.

The proper human response to such books would be faith. The Jews and the Christians, Israel and Jesus, differed about the interpretation of Old Testament Scripture but not about its origin or its authority.

The ruling power of the covenantal book

This agreement on the divine origin and authority of Scripture is a crucial point in an age when many Christians have been prepared to accord the Bible only a reduced, even human-only, status. If we wish to worship Jesus Christ as our Lord, his words will already have authority for us. But his teaching showed such respect for the origin and authority of Scripture that we will add the Old Testament to his words. Likewise, we will add the words of the apostles whom he appointed and to whom he promised his Spirit as their teacher and guide. In short, submission to Jesus as Lord brings with it submission to a covenantal book which we must call the word of God.

Such a result conforms with God's whole method of dealing with his people to that juncture. It would be astonishing if God changed his method of ruling his people, given that from the very first his word was the point of issue. Nor can we avoid this conclusion by arguing that this merely formed part of the cultural context in which Jesus lived without endorsing it. On the contrary, here is the culture which he plainly believed had been specifically prepared for his coming by God. Furthermore, he was perfectly prepared to be critical of aspects of the current theology, but to him 'scripture cannot be broken' (Jn. 10:35).

If we follow the clue that the Scriptures are a covenantal book and the covenant is God's means of ruling his people it will help our approach to the Bible. There are some ways of thinking about the Bible which turn it into a thoroughly didactic book filled with doctrinal statements. We ask only 'What does the Bible teach?' and are frustrated when it seems to teach little. But a covenantal book prepared for the wise rule of God's people by God will meet their needs in a variety of ways, and its provision will come in different forms – wisdom, psalm, apocalyptic writing, poetry, gospel, letter. It reflects the many-sidedness of God's relationship with us, while at the same time constantly reminding us that he is a God who promises and fulfils.

Aspects of the covenant book

Truth

To accept the authority of Jesus is to accept the ruling authority of God's covenantal word. A relationship has been established. The words which create the relationship and define its terms cannot be refused or put aside. We may question what such words mean, but the very nature of the one who has become our God indicates that we are to trust his promises and keep his will. All this is implied when we speak of the Bible as inspired by God and infallible. We mean that it is God's gift and expresses his authority. We mean that it will not deceive us or mislead us, that it is completely trustworthy, that it is true.

Such an understanding of the Bible does not ignore its human features. It is like the prophet who is inspired, or like the speech of Jesus himself as reported in the four Gospels. It must be attributed completely to God and completely to the human author if we are to do justice to its reality. It bears the ordinary marks of ordinary language. It is lively, evocative and imaginative. Approximations abound; so do similes, metaphors and other figures of speech; pre-scientific descriptions occur; quotations from non-biblical sources; generalizations; infelicities of speech; interpretations of things that were said and done. The humanness of its language does not entail error and deception, however, any more than the humanness of Jesus entailed deceptive error in his speech or deeds.

Real difficulties remain in Scripture, however, not least because we have only copies and not the original text. Nonetheless, I still believe that it is important not to accept the charge of error for two chief reasons, one theological and the second practical. My first reason is that the origin of the text is the work of God's Spirit. I am uneasy with a view that professes to distinguish between infallible truths of faith and life which are taught by the Holy Spirit, and errors of fact and history which are human mistakes. In Scripture the meaning is bound up with the facts. Secondly, I believe that when we take the view that there are errors in Scripture, we tend to slide over the difficult texts and passages. We then fail to give vigorous exegesis the attention it deserves and we become unwilling to listen to the testimony of the whole Bible in seeking to know and be ruled by God.

Function

Another issue is also at stake. The covenantal book is not simply a textbook, even a textbook of theology. It is the word of God and hence it is the very instrument by which God rules us. To trust his word is to trust him; to obey his word is to obey him; to learn from his word is to learn from him. Through Scripture a pure and wholesome language becomes the medium of the most important relationship that we could ever have. It is the exact point on which faith rests. To encourage a habitual doubt in regard to Scripture, to treat it as the word of man in the midst of which may be found the word of God, is to emasculate faith itself; to attack God's method of ruling us. It is at this point that God becomes remote, and we are tempted to meet him in ways which are satisfactory only in our imagination. It is at this point, necessarily, that true assurance ebbs away.

Relationships can flourish only in the sphere of truth. Liars are very poor friends. We must be able to trust our language or else communion cannot occur. Christianity can be weak only when the word of God is lost. Our theological education will be affected, followed by our preaching and our Christian education. Then faith itself will become thin or disappear, for it has not got truth in words to feed on. The very health of God's people depends upon acceptance of the authority of the Bible.

Centre

But what of Christ, the Word, image and Son of God? Is he not the centre point of revelation? Is truth not a person rather than a set of words, however venerable? We must reply, first, that Christ is, indeed, the focus of revelation. His coming is the central point of the Bible and it is from him and from his perspective that we must interpret the whole Bible. Thus the Old Testament requirements for the people of God living in Canaan as a nation were transformed when, under the new covenant, that people became international. We then see that our homeland is the age to come, our temple is Christ himself, and our sacrifice is his cross. The key to all this is that the Bible itself provides the authorized interpretation of the Bible.

There is another side to this, however. The Jesus Christ we know comes to us in words, the words of the Bible. This Jesus is the Jesus we have access to and we must be wary of the sentimental or sceptical alternatives. He is the centre of the Bible; the Bible defines who he is. Not only is it right to say that Jesus is God's revelation; to be true to him we must say that the Bible is God's revelation, that its propositions are not somehow opposed to his person, but are the means by which we worship him in trusting obedience. And because Jesus is God's Word, his greatest and ultimate self-revelation before the final unveiling at the end of history, the Bible is the complete and sufficient revelation of God for our time. The faith has once for all been delivered to God's people (Jude 3), and the practice of adding to the Bible contemporary or even traditional 'revelations' or interpretations, however exciting, however venerable, serves only to diminish Scripture, because it diminishes Christ who is God's great Word to men and women.

Renewing our language

When speaking in defence of Hardy's god, I noted the problem that we have with language. Is it a fit vehicle of communication between persons? Can human words speak of the invisible God? Has language been corrupted?

My argument is that Jesus Christ, the image and Word of God, meets these difficulties. In him we have the one who is both God and man, offering true revelation as a word and in words that we can comprehend and trust. If, following him, we regard the Bible as the word of God, we can draw two conclusions.

Firstly, we have been provided with a God-accredited language as a fitting vehicle for relationship with him. Both the preaching of the gospel, and the Scriptures which incorporate the gospel, claim to be the truth and to relate us to God and to one another. They demonstrate that words in their natural meaning are adequate to convey the most profound of truths.

Secondly, it follows that the language we use with each other can also be endorsed as a fit vehicle for relationship. Since our communion with God uses language without embarrassment, so, too, may our fellowship with one another. The Bible also makes a powerful assault on all dishonest and corrupt speech, however, demanding truth and sincerity. Taken seriously it can cleanse speech and create truth and love. Our personhood, like God's, is bound up with relationships based on the communication that comes through language.

If, however, theologians are able to give the Bible only a human status – as a witness to God's word, for example – relationship with God is lost. The church will founder and we will experience the awful judgment of Amos: a famine 'of hearing the words of the Lord' (Am. 8:11). This, alas, seems to be the situation in many contemporary churches. Christians have failed to see how integral the word of God in Scripture is to the very way in which God chooses to rule over his people. Having lost confidence in God's word, they find only the remote god of Thomas Hardy, dark and dumb. I believe that only the rehabilitation and exposition of the Bible will give confidence to the church about God and, further, that it may help rejuvenate speech in our society, for this is the way God rules over us.

To discuss or think about

1 Why is it important to understand Jesus Christ as the fulfilment of a nation's history?
2 How does the story of Israel, as a nation based on a covenant and governed by covenant words, point forward to the End in God's purposes?
3 Why does 'submission to Jesus as Lord (bring) with it submission to a covenantal book which we must call the word of God'?
4 How should Christians regard the Bible?

Conclusion to part 3

When the Word became flesh in the person of Jesus
Christ he chose to do so in the womb of a virgin, Mary of
Nazareth. We are not told that a virginal conception was
necessary for the incarnation. Given the pattern of significant events surrounding the birth and early lives of previous saviours like Moses, however, we may at least read
it as a great sign, and, given that he is both God and man,
an appropriate sign of his coming.

The message of Immanuel, 'God with us', continues to
lodge in the sentimental faith of millions for whom the rest
of Christianity makes no sense at all. Thomas Hardy knew
the pull of this story, even for an unbelieving heart. In a
poem he makes use of an old legend that at midnight on
Christmas Eve the cattle in their stables all kneel, as you
may imagine the animals did long ago in that stable where
Jesus was born. For, if indeed God would deign to visit us
in this weary world, and visit us as a tiny child, and live
with us, what could we then not face? What could we then
not hope? What could ever steal away our joy?

> Christmas Eve, and twelve of the clock
> Now they are all on their knees,
> An elder said as we sat in a flock
> By the ember in hearthside ease . . .

He pictures a friend creeping out to see the animals
kneeling and, moved, imagines that he would go too.

> ... I should go with him in the gloom
> Hoping it might be so.[1]

There is our choice. The god that we imagine, 'the dreaming, dark, dumb Thing that turns the handle of this idle Show', or the true God who has not left us in such solitary confinement but who speaks, who relates, who is personal; the true God who came down to earth and lived among us full of grace and truth. '*Hoping* it might be so'? Immanuel! God is with us, indeed!

PART FOUR

A declaration of peace

At eleven o'clock on the morning of 11 November 1918, the combatants of the First World War ceased fighting. At 9.15 that morning, an officer, Lieutenant-Colonel Bernard Freyberg, VC, heard that all hostilities were to finish in less than two hours. The carnage, destruction and misery were almost over. You may imagine that most soldiers would have spent those two hours ensuring that they did not become the last, senseless victims of the horror. Freyberg, however, did not. In a letter to Winston Churchill he wrote,

> I had a most wonderful finish to my war ... I decided to get in touch with the Bosche (*sic*) and raid him with my Cavalry and cyclists one last time ... We started at 9.50 and galloped 20 kilometres, rushed his outpost lines at the gallop at 5 minutes to eleven and charged into the village only 9 strong shooting up the streets with revolvers and chasing Bosche round blocks of buildings. We captured a bridge head at 2 minutes to eleven and mopped up the village to the tune of 4 officers, 102 other ranks and several machine guns.

The Germans protested; Freyberg was given another medal. The hero himself concluded his note to Churchill, 'I thought this would amuse you.'[1]

Two minutes after Freyberg's exploit, on the eleventh hour of the eleventh day of the eleventh month, the 'monstrous anger of the guns' and the 'shrill, demented choirs of wailing shells' were silenced at last.[2] Everywhere, men and women hoped fervently for a new era of justice, love and peace. The Freyberg incident suggests how vain such hopes were to be. The attitudes which created the war in the first place – rivalry, racism, greed, aggrandizement, fear – remained, as they remain to this day. The poisoned legacy of the war was injustice. Fighting ceased, navies were scrapped, soldiers sent home, but true peace could not come.

As this bloody century ends, we are heartened by the end of the Cold War. But this contraction does not constitute an unambiguous outbreak of peace. The retreat has left exposed the old, bitter conflicts and injustices of Europe which had been effectively masked in the era of the superpowers. The Baltic states, the Slavic peoples, the Turks and Armenians, Arabs and Israelis all have their claims and counterclaims. Aspects of the war against Iraq may be traced back to decisions made in and after the First World War by the victorious allies. While injustice is felt we do not have peace.

Christians are not surprised by this. It is true that the Bible itself holds out the hope of a wonderful era of real peace. The Bible also exposes human sinfulness, injustice and pride, however, teaching that while such things exist so, too, will war and human cruelty. Our quarrel with God has led to our quarrels with one another. The Bible's hope for real peace rests on a far deeper thing than human diplomacy. The Bible calls for such justice that a complete revolution is involved: pre-eminently a revolution in the relationship between human beings and God. Furthermore, since human effort is so inadequate, such a revolution must come from God himself. Our only hope is that he will declare and create peace with justice. Our only hope is that this is involved in the End that he has planned.

It is, of course, a real question as to whether people like us should enter a new order of justice. Surely only the just may do so. It is, however, the triumph of the love that is at the heart of the universe that such a miracle is possible. To see how this can be so, in the next three chapters, we will focus once again on Jesus Christ, the Servant King. Our method remains that of studying the great central person of the Bible, once again beginning at the End, as we think first of his future, then his past, and finally of his present. As we see him in this way, we will see ourselves and understand who and where we are, what has been done for us and what we must do. In him we will perceive our own past, our own present and our own future.

CHAPTER 9

The Servant King: his future work

Jesus Christ the Judge

The Bible tells us that at some future time Jesus Christ will act as 'judge of the living and the dead' (Acts 10:42). The era of peace will be ushered in by justice, the righting of wrong, the reward of goodness, the punishment of evil. This is at the heart of Jesus' future, although there is much more to it than that. In an earlier chapter I indicated how this future moment of truth actually serves now to reveal the significance of human life, its importance to God. Our words, our thoughts, our character, our failures all matter to him, and the Bible speaks unashamedly of reward and punishment, of wages and debt.

The last word, 'debt', is particularly significant. Jesus himself uses it to portray the situation of human beings before God, and he has no hesitation in presuming that the debt we owe personally is of such massive proportions that the income of a whole nation would be insufficient to repay it. No other metaphor could more strongly convey our hopelessness on the one hand and our wrongness on the other. We cannot pay, but we ought to pay. Whatever others may let us get away with through weakness or apathy, God is not mocked. Our capacity to evade responsibility for evil is not permanent. God is a righteous God and, in the universe as he has created it, there is right and wrong and responsibility, no matter what we think. There can be no peace without justice, and the future of Jesus Christ contains God's pledge that justice will one day be done. But, then, who among us can stand?

Loss of moral framework

Our contemporaries, however, are bewildered by talk that includes such concepts as debt, judgment and objective guilt. These categories seem to have slipped into obscurity as though they are no longer useful to describe human behaviour or persons. Their disappearance is only apparent, however. It is a mark of the confusion of our time that we have to continue to appeal to them even when we do not use the words explicitly. The consequence of our confusion is vulnerability to manipulation, and doubt about our own worth. We have lost the moral framework which enables us to discriminate, to judge.

Attitudes to anger illustrate the point. We are constantly advised to express our anger for the sake of mental hygiene. If owning our anger, punching pillows and yelling in private do not relieve stress, a carefully controlled approach to an anger-inducing person is advised. 'I am feeling angry with you and I would like to tell you why,' is a courteous form of words. Good manners then dictate that we receive at least some form of consent from the other party before we begin our emotional cleansing and, hopefully, reconciliation.

There is no especial harm in all this except where it avoids explicit *moral* thought. We need to be encouraged to ask, 'Am I right to be angry?' In fact, if we do discuss our anger with an offending person, it would not be long before the question would arise. We invariably wish to justify our approach. We wish to demonstrate that the other person was in the wrong or to modify our response by agreeing that they were innocent. When a person says, 'I am feeling angry towards you and I would like to tell you why,' you know for sure that you are about to be blamed for a perceived fault. Your options are to confess it or refute it. In any case, there is an implicit appeal to a moral standard, a moral framework. If you judge yourself to be guilty, or at fault, you owe a debt to the other person which needs to be discharged by confession and, where necessary, amendment and restitution.

We do not speak in these terms, however. The capacity to think explicitly like this seems to have been lost, with a twofold effect on us. Firstly, it makes the Christian message difficult to understand because it deals with realities for which there appears to be no language. Secondly, it distorts human relationships because, in fact, we cannot get on without such categories.

Take the task of being a parent. Under the impact of popular psychological teaching, parents have gained the impression that children are activated by a set of inner drives which are basically instinctual but can be modified, crushed or diverted by nature. Although we all have some inner freedom, we are very largely shaped by the interaction of instinct and nurture. The parent needs to provide the context in which the person will mature and be well balanced, independent, creative, positive, free from self-doubt without being arrogant. In this task encouragement is central; positive reinforcement is worth ten times as much as negativity. Better to tell a child, 'That was nearly right,' rather than 'That was wrong.' Do not allow competition, except competition with one's self: 'You are reading well' means better than you were reading last week, rather than better than your peers, or the norm for your age or, heaven forbid! 'accurately and with expression' or some other quasi-objective remark. To encourage, to motivate, to create positive feelings – these things will work for you.

Now all this is true enough, and a vast improvement over negative and discipline-fixated ways of nurturing children. Left on its own, however, it has every chance of blunting moral sensibility, for it refuses to allow reality, moral or physical, to carry much weight. It is not, of course, that we prevent the human propensity to blame others or to find a scapegoat or to feel guilty. But since we tone down or remove the capacity for moral judgment, we turn these into functions of the emotional life and invent the little courtesies of anger that I described. Our relationships with one another are deprived of an important aspect of reality.

The consequences of a lack of a moral framework can also be seen in the matter of divorce. There can be no doubt that the situation before the current matrimonial legislation was hypocritical and farcical. Since these aspects were linked with some attempt by the law to apportion blame, it was felt wise to move as far as possible to 'no fault' divorce. Once again, it is not altogether unhealthy for us to remind ourselves that blame for the breakdown of human relationships is not easy to apportion, even by the participants; indeed, given what we know about human drives, nurture and personality, blame and responsibility are not always the proper categories to adopt. But, when every allowance has been made and every concession to the need for a positive approach, the virtual absence of a moral perspective is tragic. It robs the participants of self-knowledge. It robs them of the capacity for informed and balanced judgments concerning others and leaves them only with their feelings. It creates a vulnerability to inordinate guilt-feelings about their own contribution to marital discord. Above all, it stands like an impenetrable barrier to the cleansing and renewing power of forgiveness asked for and granted. We can only ask for forgiveness when we recognize that we are in the wrong.

Of course, modern attitudes are not, in fact, new at all. Faced with the Bible's uncompromising moral demands, three responses may be detected over the years. The first is to lower the standards, not usually by frontal attack but by so emphasizing the trivial that the major aspect is neglected; or, in another favourite ploy, by providing a loophole. In other words, to declare that 'fault' or 'sin' do not exist. The second response is to declare that the sinner does not exist, by arguing that we can be blamed only for what we could have done or avoided given our nature and, hence, since it is our nature to sin, our sin is not wrong. The third response is to blame someone else entirely. In Christian history – in fact, since Eve onwards – this has often been the devil, although notice that Adam blamed both God and Eve!

By these evasions, ancient or modern, we cheat others and we cheat ourselves. Thus it is that we regard sin as some people regard illness; by declaring that it is an illusion and cannot hurt us. Such a response suits the temper of social liberalism with its easy creed that I do no wrong as long as I do not actually harm anyone. It helpfully lowers the temperature, or appears to. In giving the impression that we do not require moral categories in everyday life, however, it encourages undiscriminating freedom of expression (which is bondage not liberty), personal insecurity and inability to judge oneself effectively. It is also unreal, since even the most liberal person is morally intolerant and righteously indignant at some point – a 'liberal fascist', as I heard one person describe herself recently when seeking compulsory sex education in school. Most important of all, it does not equip us for the future where we will experience a judgment based on rigorous moral principles.

The enduring reality of justice and guilt

Two great elements of moral thinking can be banished neither from this world, nor from the future: justice and guilt. Even in a minor personal confrontation you ask yourself, 'Is this person right to be angry? Am I at fault?' These are the very issues that will also arise in the End before the throne of God.

Justice

In Christian terms, the source of justice is not some independent principle in the universe but neither is it an arbitrary whim of God. It arises from the steadfast nature of God himself. Justice is God's consistent goodness. The Bible itself says that God cannot lie and cannot deny himself. It does not mean that we have a limited God who has to bow to external forces of morality. It means that the true God is true; that if he were to lie he would no longer be himself. He cannot lie. He is absolutely consistent and reliable. It is part of his power that no other power in the universe can make him be other than consistent and, in fact, consistently, overflowingly good. We may be sure, furthermore, that God's goodness has at its essence the love he has for others.

In our experience the world is a difficult and unruly place. The Bible describes nature itself as 'subjected to futility' and 'groaning' (Rom. 8:20, 22), and human beings as sinful and rebellious. But the turbulent forces of decay and dissent do not compromise God's justice, his consistent goodness. They are under his control, and in his own perfect way and his own good time he is bringing peace and righteousness to pass. The frustration of the creation is according to his will, and its 'groaning' points to the liberation it is going to experience as it shares 'the glorious liberty of the children of God' (Rom. 8:21). At every point we encounter the God who is gracious in his justice.

Now consider what this signifies about justice. When God acts justly we can be sure of the complete consistency of his treatment. He will not favour one above the other, or wink at the sins of one while chastising the sins of the other. He will condemn, reward, punish and recompense with justice. What he says he will do, he will do. With God we may be sure of a scrupulous fairness and even-handedness. The Bible declares that he cannot be bribed, that is, he cannot be diverted by irrelevant considerations from treating us fairly. A good God cannot be less.

A good God must be more, however. Even in human justice we demand equity with justice in order that justice may be done, and this is a pale reflection of the love that motivates God's justice. For true justice will express his loving goodness, and the loving goodness of God is re-creating his rule over all the world, bringing right out of wrong, bringing joy out of pain, bringing liberty out of bondage, bringing to pass a new heaven and a new earth, creating peace with justice.

In the Bible, his justice, or consistent goodness, is referred to as his 'righteousness' in order to bring out the dynamic quality of his good purposes. God's righteousness is the source of the Bible's good news. That God is both consistent and good creates hope. What such a God has done in and for his rebellious world is the glad tidings, which bring peace and joy. We may trust him to have fulfilled his promises and brought salvation into the world.

Equity does not involve equality at all points. God is not bound by equity to treat all identically, any more than it bound him to create all identically. Justice is not inconsistent with the subordination of persons to each other, for example. When even-handedness has been accomplished, grace may choose to act in accordance with good purposes, for justice is the consistent goodness of God. In this way, variety of treatment and of status may occur under God's just rule.

Guilt

Guilt is overwhelming when confronted with justice. Our conscience is a barometer of guilt, but an ineffective one.

The conscience is formed by a variety of factors in human experience and may give totally false information about the content of right and wrong. The Bible sees it more as a painful, accusing (and sometimes excusing) inner voice after the event rather than a voice to consult for guidance before decisions are taken. As such it may be coarsened to such an extent that it will excuse our sins, or it may be sensitive to such an extent that it will accuse us concerning harmless behaviour. Excessive guilt-feelings related to real or imaginary faults can be quite disabling and may need psychiatric help. If, however, such therapists suggest that sin is not sin, in an attempt to soothe the conscience, they may accomplish short-term benefit (though I have some doubt even here) at the expense of long-term blessedness.

There is the inner guilt-feeling and there is also the fact of objective guilt. Inner guilt reveals something about the nature of objective guilt. It forces confession of failure in order to acknowledge and share the guilt with one who can help sustain the burden of it, and it seeks punishment in order to relieve the pain through penalty. In other words, it shows us that something must be done about guilt, and its urge to confession and penalty indicates what this is. Objective guilt attracts an authoritative declaration of failure from the judge (in the case of sin from God himself) and the creation of a debt to be paid or a recompense to be made. Guilt is unfinished moral business. The fact that in this life we incur a thousand times more debt than we are conscious of, especially debt to God whose laws we are breaking, ought not to blind us to reality.

In sum, when we consider the future work of Jesus Christ, the Bible takes us to the last day, the judgment, and places us there before the throne of God. Our twentieth-century experience, that peace must be founded on justice, is true of the way God runs the universe. If we are to have peace, it must come through justice. But our conscience, inadequate though it is, warns us of the facts about ourselves. We are not so much afraid to die as ashamed to die. We see that the rebellion against God of which we are part will not be overcome at the stroke of a pen. Great unfinished moral obligation is at stake. There is nothing, not even the whole world itself, with which we could bribe God or ransom our own lives, let alone the lives of others.

It is all very well, then, for me to portray the wonders of the future as I did in the first chapter, the 'new heaven and a new earth in which righteousness dwells', as Peter calls it (2 Pet. 3:13). We will be excluded from it for ever, as unrighteous. If this problem is to be met, it is God who must do it; only he can create peace with justice. In chapter 7 I indicated that our Creator has indeed joined us, that the Word became flesh and dwelt among us. In the next chapter we will focus on what he went on to do when he became man, we will see what God has done and what Jesus Christ did to secure the salvation of lost and guilty sinners.

To discuss or think about

1 What problems does modern thought have with concepts of debt, judgment and objective guilt?
2 What does the Bible mean by justice and guilt?

CHAPTER 10

The Servant King: his past work

There is joy and hope on almost every page of the New Testament because of Jesus Christ. 'Christ Jesus came into the world,' writes Paul, 'to save sinners' (1 Tim. 1:15), and the wonder of it all still grips readers today. Jesus Christ died most terribly, but he was no failure, no victim. The manner of his life was extraordinary. His teaching surpassed all others. By his death he brought forgiveness, love, salvation, justice and peace. His death crowned his work and was his victory. These three elements, his life, his teaching and his death, constitute the work that he did for us. Let us now consider them in turn.

The manner of his life

The Bible is notably reserved about the life of Jesus. It gives us no physical description of him. It leaves whole stretches of time about which nothing is said. It omits mention of things which we would regard as basic to our appreciation of a person. It says nothing at all, for example, about whether he was married. Other facts, such as his age, have to be gleaned from incidental references or deduced from a hint or suggestion. We have no insight into matters of intense interest in our age such as the psychology of Jesus. Despite the many attempts since the eighteenth century, there is not enough material about Jesus to write a biography in the modern sense.

That is not to say, however, that his life is of no consequence and that we should pass straight on to a consideration of his teaching. On the contrary, it matters in four ways. Firstly, it matters as an example. It is not an example in the sense that it will give guidance for handling every situation. But it is an example of the spirit of the servant, who served ultimately in his death for others. All of us are called to adopt the pattern of his service. Secondly, it matters as an incarnation. It is essential to the salvation offered through Jesus that his human life was a genuine one, that he was not pseudo-human. He had to pass through our growth and our trials; he had to become the head of our race. Thirdly, his life is important because it was sinless. Again and again the Bible says of Jesus what it says of no-one else, even its greatest heroes: this man was without sin. He had to be truly man to save us, but no sinful man could save, for then he himself would have been in need of salvation. Fourthly, his life shows him as the victor over Satan. We have the memorable picture of Jesus being tempted at the beginning of the Gospels. The story is not given in order to teach us how to defeat temptation but as a tribute to the one who did defeat it and went on defeating it to the end. The story should create thanksgiving before emulation.

There is a further reason why his life matters, however, a reason that is hard to describe but true nonetheless. Despite all the gaps and puzzles about his life, when all is said and done, and the four Gospels are studied to see what they reveal about the person who dominates them, millions of people over the years have been persuaded that this human life was the life of one who was the Son of God, God with us. If you were to ask what is the secret of this capacity to persuade (which is manifestly not a creation of the Gospel writers) I would say that it was in the way he treated people, in his sharpness in the face of religious cant, in his courage before political adversaries, in his sternness with his wayward disciples, in his tender encouragement of the weak and fallen. I would say that, of the terms of abuse and vilification which he endured, one in particular says what sort of man he was: 'Look', they said, '... a friend of sinners!' (Lk. 7:34). Here, indeed, was the life that God might lead should he come among us.

The power of his teaching

Showing tourists around a city is a strange experience. As often as not they are looking the wrong way; at least they fail to see what is really there. They pretend to be impressed, but do not know what they are looking at. It takes time to see a city in its own context, to study the texture of the buildings, to see how the landscape has been dealt with, to appreciate the achievement.

Thus it is with the teaching of Jesus. Those who have heard of its strength and beauty and visit the New Testament as tourists will not be impressed. They will not see what the fuss is about. It is in a strange language, it deals with alien issues, its parables are not really stories, it is highly selective in its topics. The tourist will recognize a few-well known landmarks, be consoled and be grateful to report that the journey has been made and the Sermon on the Mount is still in place.

Those who stay and ponder, those who turn it over and study, those who look at it from different perspectives, those who take the trouble to find out what this kingdom of God is and what eternal life is, those who set the words into their context, will get a very different impression, however. The fact that the words are time-bound is part of their power. They relate specifically and cuttingly to their context so that they may do the same in ours when we take the trouble to let them work on us. They are particular because an exhaustive commentary on life would never be complete and would accomplish the wrong thing. That they are pithy is part of their cutting-edge. Indeed, there is no part of life or death into which a word from Jesus will not find its way with light and challenge.

There is beauty in these words, there is humour, there is irony and sarcasm. There is the brilliant, unforgettable metaphor; there are majestic words, there are words of obscurity; there are words that tease and irritate, that call for a totality of commitment which we sense is boundless; there are words of consolation and strength; there are polemical words that almost take your breath away with their sharpness. There are words and phrases which have actually shaped our language, and many other languages, too – the good Samaritan, the prodigal son, the fatted calf, the Pharisee, the signs of the times, the eye of the needle, hypocrite.

Indeed, Jesus said that you could build your whole life on his words and even the earthquake and the tempest would never bring you down. Yet whoever comes to these words expecting a philosophy of life or a pathway of moral excellence will go away unsatisfied. They are too apocalyptic for that – they are like the words of a man who speaks as he climbs an active volcano, conscious that the end could come at any time. Jesus was a preacher, a reporter, a herald, not a philosopher or an ethicist. He argued and urged and exhorted and warned those who were on the slopes with him. It was the crisis of the occasion which produced the extraordinary language, not the quiet and contemplative life in a cave or a library. He had a kingdom to announce.

There is one more feature of the words and this, too, is apparent in Jesus' saying about the earthquake and the storm and the foundation being his words. How does it happen that such words spoken so long ago and under such circumstances should continue to have power today? I believe it is because they have as their inner strength the One who uttered them. In the end, they turn out to be words about him, words that reveal him to us, words which clothe him and give us access to him, words through which he rules over us. If you think of Jesus as the great ethics teacher you will repudiate his words apart from a few sayings you may be fond of. If you see who Jesus really was, however, you will be glad to have them because they are so God-like. Here, indeed, were the words that God might speak should he come among us.

The nature of his death

The life and words of Jesus are remarkable. Both are essential to the work he did. We come now, however, to the centre of all – and the most awesome subject of all – the rejection, betrayal, torture, trial and crucifixion of the Son of God. Of all the themes in the New Testament, this one dominates. The story of the Gospels is less the story of his life than the story of what led up to his death, and the Bible does not treat his death as simply a terrible fate that befell a good man from which we may draw lessons about human nature and the problem of suffering. In the Bible's terms, it was something he did, not something he endured; it was the captain joining the life raft and bringing it to safety. Amazingly, it was the judge undergoing judgment. Thus we must discuss not so much the nature or circumstances of his death as the meaning and achievement of it. How does his past work of dying transform his future work of judging? How does the injustice which he suffered affect the justice which he must initiate?

It is as well to underscore the uniqueness of this event – as though it needs saying – from the beginning. The New Testament offers us a great variety of explanatory words and phrases as well as the interpretations evident in the Gospel narratives themselves. To offer a schematic account, as we must in a study of this sort, we are bound to fail to include all the nuances and, thus, to obscure as well as to enlighten. More than that, however, in this event more than any other, the resources of analogy and parallel are inadequate to describe the significance of what occurred. We may say more, much more, than some will allow, but we must exercise the caution of Moses who, at the Lord's command, removed his shoes on holy ground.

Even more now, as a matter of approach, we will benefit by moving into this with Jesus, so to speak. By asking who he was, what he achieved and, finally, what he revealed, we will discover something of how it is that the death of Jesus can be said to prepare us for the day of judgment, deal with our sins and cancel our debt.

Who he was

Four of the names and descriptions of Jesus help us here. Firstly, *he was the Son of God*. As the Son we recollect that he was one with the Father and the Spirit in all eternity; that he was sent to earth by his Father, freely and willingly entering our existence despite the cost. As the Son he is constantly and uniquely beloved of the Father. When we realize that it is the Son whose death we speak of, we see that, whatever was achieved, it was the achievement of God – the Father, the Son and the Holy Spirit – and whatever was achieved, was achieved at immense cost to God.

Secondly, *he was the Servant of the Lord*. This title goes back in time to the prophet Isaiah, who spoke of the Lord's Servant as one who would be despised and rejected, 'a man of sorrows and acquainted with grief' (Is. 53:3), but one who, in death, would be 'wounded for our transgressions' and 'bruised for our iniquities' (Is. 53:5). Jesus called himself the one who came 'not to be served but to serve' and in a reference to Isaiah 53 added '. . . and to give his life as a ransom for many' (Mk. 10:45). Jesus had already indicated the sheer impossibility of gathering enough treasure in all the world to ransom the life of one person faced with judgment (Mk. 8:37–39). Now he declares that the giving of his own life would be such a ransom exchanged for the lives of many. His death would substitute for the deaths of many.

Thirdly, *he was God's appointed High Priest.* The central task of the High Priest was to offer sacrifice to God on behalf of men to take away sin. Jesus is the High Priest, and his death is the sacrifice. His death was an offering by him to God in the Spirit of God. Animal sacrifices were very inadequate prototypes of what was aimed at here. The model of an innocent animal giving its life so that humans may be forgiven illuminates some aspects of the death of the innocent Jesus. There are massive differences, however, not least that he achieved what they could not, namely the actual removal of judgment on sin. The New Testament constantly tells us that the sacrifice of the death of Jesus offered by him on the cross was done 'for you'. It was on our behalf – more, it was in our place.

The plain result is that peace with justice becomes possible. Can we say more? The Bible regards the death of Jesus as having the ability to remove guilt and penalty. Is there any indication of how this is so? Nowhere does it suggest that it does so by making us more moral people, as though a dose of goodness could wipe out past offences. Instead the Bible connects Jesus' death with God's righteous wrath, and gives it the power to exhaust this anger. We deserve his wrath for our sins, for, fundamentally, he is the offended party. He loves us and wishes there to be peace between us, but it must be as an expression of his own consistent goodness, his just love. It would be absurd to think that the death of an animal could exempt me from the punishment I deserve; immoral to imagine that I could appoint a fellow human being to take my place in the judgment, to provide a ransom by suffering the curse due to me; impossible that there should be a true forgiveness which simply overlooked the offence without cost.

In his consistent goodness, however, God has undertaken to ensure that the penalty was sustained by one who had both the right to represent us and the capacity to pay. He, himself, in the person of the Son of God and as the offended party, has absorbed the judgment due. Forgiveness was costly, but its cost has been borne by the offended party. Justice has been done and it has brought peace.

This, it seems to me, is what the Bible says. I do not claim to understand it, except dimly. If we continue to think exclusively in categories drawn from the human experience of punishment in law courts then we shall be led astray, for the situation is as personal as it is forensic. But it seems to me to be thoroughly honouring to God's character in all its ways, to take sin and judgment with the seriousness they deserve and to meet our human need for guilt to be removed. Any explanation which does less is unworthy of what Christ achieved.

Fourthly and finally, *he was the Saviour of God's people*. God's people in Old Testament days often received their salvation in unlikely ways or from unlikely people as a reminder of the fact that it was God alone who was the Saviour. Nothing in the history of the people, however, could have quite prepared them for God's ultimate means of salvation – which was at least as ugly as an electric chair would be to us – or for God's despised and rejected Saviour.

Once more, though, this salvation far surpassed the Old Testament experience. Then, the people were released from Philistines or Egyptians or Babylonians. The work of Jesus was directed at Satan, however, whom the Bible calls 'the ruler of this world' and 'the god of this world'. The Bible pictures the human race as a whole as held in bondage in 'the kingdom of darkness', and it portrays Jesus as Saviour when, on the cross, he breaks the powerful hold of Satan through the forgiveness of sins and frees his people.

What he achieved

Already something of the achievement of the cross has become clear. It was the ransoming of doomed captives, the turning away of judgment, and the release of Satan's captives. The Bible takes us further, however, and there are four further aspects to observe if we wish to measure the grandeur of what he did.

Firstly, the cross achieved forgiveness. We have been forced to the judgment seat and heard in anticipation the adverse judgment of God on our lives. When we stand there truly and in horror at ourselves, nothing could be more precious, more overwhelming, than a word which brings forgiveness. Through Christ's death we may have the forgiveness now and always, not through some cheap method by which God simply decides to forgive, but through the method of his consistent goodness by which our debt is fully, willingly and graciously paid by another, so that it can never return to haunt us.

Secondly, the cross achieved reconciliation. The Bible calls us the enemies of God. As enemies of so powerful a being you would expect us to make the first move to him. In fact, our hostility is so deep that we refuse to do so. Imagine then the love of God, the Servant King, who himself declares not war but peace on our ungrateful heads. The Bible says, 'God was in Christ reconciling the world to himself, not counting their trespasses against them ...' (2 Cor. 5:19) and tells us that we have 'peace with God' (Rom. 5:1).

Thirdly, the cross achieved unity. Jesus' death brings peace with God. More than that, however, it brings peace between his ancient people and the new people who come from every nation under heaven and from every family as he promised Abraham. The new people would now be joined with his ancient people as one new body, the church. Christ laid down his life, the Bible says, for his sheep, for his church. By this, God has achieved a new creation, a new race of men and women to rule the world, to come under the leadership of Jesus Christ.

Fourthly, the cross achieved finality. One of the evidences that the old sacrificial system did not really work was its sheer repetitiveness. Sacrifices had to be made constantly. Such is the power of the death of Christ that it needed to occur only once; it need never be repeated; it must not be supplemented by any human endeavour, as though we need the death of Christ plus human effort to remove sin. It is perfect because he is perfect; it can cleanse perfectly the most darkened and fearful conscience.

What he revealed

If Jesus is the chief focus of God's whole revelation of himself, the cross is the point at which the light shines brightest. Consider what we may see here as nowhere else.

Firstly, our redemption cost the death of the Son of God and he was the victim of sin and Satan. The cross shows both the extent of human depravity and the seriousness with which God takes our sin. It shows us the nature of kingly service and rebukes us for our own inadequacies in this regard.

Secondly, our lives before God depend not on something we do for him but something unique that he has done for us. We need his forgiveness from start to finish and can never graduate beyond the cross and its power to cleanse us. Furthermore, it is the motive for the Christian life and especially for our obligation to forgive others who offend against us.

Thirdly, in the cross we discover that the Son of God understands more of suffering from the inside than we could ever have believed, that he has been tested on every point as we are and yet was without sin.

Finally, there is no better vantage point to comprehend God's love than the cross of Christ. Father, Son and Spirit, as ever united, were graciously determined to save a world that was hostile and rebellious. When our own interpretation of the world leads us to doubt God's love, it is to the cross that we must look for reassurance and hope. When the Bible wants to emphasize his love it does so, not with some appeal to a lofty metaphysical principle, but to the grime and horror and blood of the crucifixion, to history. Of this, Paul can even allow us to be entirely personal, when he says for us all, 'the Son of God, who loved me and gave himself for me . . .' (Gal. 2:20). With such a Saviour we need not fear things present or things to come, even when we stand before the judgment seat. For he who judges is he who has died for us. This is at the heart of the universe.

I have already observed that both the life and the teaching of Jesus demonstrate what God may indeed be like should he come among us. I have not been able to touch on the Gospel stories of his death, with his dignity, his power, his love for others, even leading to the prayer that his tormentors may be forgiven. But, taken with the goal he was set to achieve – the salvation of his enemies – this, too, forces us to ask, 'If God did come among us, would he not die like this?'

To discuss or think about

1 Despite the incomplete data on the life of Jesus, why does the story of his life matter?
2 How should we regard his teaching?
3 What made Jesus' death different from any other, however notable? What did it achieve for us?
4 What are some practical implications of the cross?

CHAPTER 11

The Servant King: his present work

The moment which sets the path for all history is the death of Jesus. It is the pledge that peace with justice is certain to arrive when Jesus comes again. In the meantime, however, Jesus is not idle. He is working towards the fulfilment of his kingdom of peace and justice.

The present work of Jesus began with his resurrection from the dead. He is now Lord of this age and the new age which has already begun. He rules over it by his Word, which is being preached by his servants and by his Spirit. When we describe his present work, therefore, we do so in terms of his resurrection, his Lordship, his Word and his Spirit. Once again we note the usefulness of viewing Christ's work from the standpoint of God's ultimate purposes, the End.

The resurrection of Jesus Christ

The cross represents the judgment of Satan, sin and the world against Christ and, indeed, in some way, the judgment of God, too. The whole business of his trials before the authorities, both Jewish and Roman, was the necessary formalization of the world's unrelenting hostility towards God's kingdom and its King. Nor can we blame others, for we recognize ourselves only too clearly in those who mouthed the adverse judgments on that day and in those who abandoned him and fled in cowardice and betrayal.

There was no way, however, in the world of God's consistent goodness, that this judgment would be permitted to stand. The New Testament resonates with the belief that, after three days, Jesus was raised from death by God as an act of triumphant vindication. The 'No' of the cross was replaced by the 'Yes' of the resurrection, and the cowardice and collapse of the disciples were transformed into a courageous and inspired witness to what they had seen and heard.

Or, that is what they said. That something happened to launch the tiny group of believers into the world, preaching the extraordinary message of a crucified and risen Saviour, no-one doubts. It is easier to believe that they were sincere about what they said than that they were liars or frauds. According to them, it was the resurrection, and they had been appointed witnesses to the reality of a person who had been thoroughly dead re-entering the door to history from the other side and living among them, not as a ghost but as an embodied, resurrected man – not simply as a resuscitated corpse (extraordinary though that may be) but as the appointed King of God's kingdom. For what they were witnessing to was that this present age and the age to come had met in Jesus – he now belonged to both worlds.

I have argued that Jesus Christ as the Word become flesh is God's great revelation to the world. If you wish to know God you will find him here. I suggested in an earlier chapter that the assessment of who Jesus is could follow three main paths, and I should indicate that we have now reached the point where I have touched on all three. The first is the question of whether he was the true fulfilment of the promises of God found in the old covenant. The second is the study of his life, teaching and death, asking whether indeed God has come among us. The third is the historical reality or otherwise of his resurrection. It is not that a resurrection on its own would reveal his identity (for there are other resurrections recorded in the Bible), but it is the resurrection of this man which is the 'Yes' of God over his life that we must consider.

It is not my present task to take us further into these questions. For that you can read the Gospels yourselves and listen to the evangelists, the preachers and the apologists. But even there, in the end, the decision you come to about the Son of God will be your own responsibility, for it involves far more than dispassionate discussion, it involves your whole person, the shape and future of your life and what you are prepared to commit. As part of that, I have been trying to outline the whole story so that you can see that it makes sense within itself and as an interpretation of human experience. In fact, it is only when you decide that Jesus is the light of the world, as he claimed, and you commit yourself to him that the whole Bible will become the Lord's covenant with you, his method of ruling over you by his word. You will have entered his kingdom. You will have entered the future.

Acknowledging the two ages

For the moment, of course, the present age and the future age mix and mingle. Indeed, the Christian would say that the two ages war with one another and that he or she is one of the main battlefields. The Bible regards the decisive fact of the present time to be that Jesus Christ now reigns over the world as its Lord. He is the man who fulfils the promise to the human race that it should have dominion. But the sinful and satanic corruption of the world remains apparent, with Christ's kingdom and the kingdom of darkness in conflict until the end of history. The danger is, for believer as well as unbeliever, that we will fail to recognize the significance of the days in which we live and so mistake our opportunities and obligations.

Thus, for example, to be convinced that Christ has withdrawn (or that there is no Christ, no Lord) and that evil is unchecked and rampant, is to give way to cynicism and despair. In this age we do have Christ's presence and his ordering of the world for good. In this age we have the joyful and sustaining news that sins are forgiven and so the future is assured. In this age we have the privilege of knowing God as Father. In this age Christ's presence assists our personal combat with sin. In this age we have the blessing of a deep union with our fellow believers. In this age we have the direction of the Scriptures by which Christ rules us. In this age we can challenge and improve the social structures by which humanity is sustained.

On the other hand, it is equally wrong to anticipate the future, to move heaven to earth, the new Jerusalem to London or Sydney. Christ has not yet destroyed all his enemies, the last of which is death. Enthusiasm for perfect Christian lives now, or physical wholeness, or financial prosperity or perfectly just societies is premature, despite the intimations we may have of them. When God promises that all things will work together for good, he defines 'the good' as being in the image of Christ (Rom. 8:28–29). For this to occur he warns us there may well be for us the same path of suffering and rejection that Christ the Saviour walked. These issues will be taken up more fully in part 5, 'Life in two worlds'.

The Lordship of Christ and his gifts of Word and Spirit

Close to the heart of what I have been talking about is the question of whether Christ is present or absent from the world. I have said that he is present with us, ordering the world for good and assisting our fight against sin. The New Testament, however, clearly and specifically records his absence as an event in history. For at the end of forty days of resurrection appearances he decisively withdrew; he ascended to heaven and cut the bond with the disciples. Then, apart from one or two extraordinary appearances, he was visible no more.

The disciples, and so all believers, were not, in fact, deprived of his presence, however. Once more an historical event at the Feast of Pentecost marks a new beginning, in a sense, the formal opening of the new age of Christ. His reign as Lord can be dated from then and his first great act was to send forth the Spirit of God, who would henceforth be present with all who believed in the Lord Jesus.

A great theologian, John Calvin, forces us to realize the significance of this. He writes, 'As long as Christ remains outside of me, and we are separated from him, all that he has suffered and done for the salvation of the human race remains useless and of no value to us.'[1] Christ continues his saving work by uniting his people to himself. Without this bonding we would not be saved; without Christ's work in bonding us, we would resist salvation. Thus it is that the mighty ministry of Christ's Spirit surrounds the whole course of our salvation: bringing us the word of Christ; bringing us to Christ in his word; bringing us to conformity to Christ; bringing us to union with the people of Christ; bringing us to the Father of Christ.

Arrangements had been made by Jesus, of course, for the preaching that he had begun to be continued. He had chosen his apostles who were to be the unrepeatable foundation group. They were the accredited eye-witnesses to his life, his teaching, his death and his resurrection and it is their testimony which gives authority to the writings of the New Testament. The communication of the word of God, however, which was now, in particular, the word that Jesus is Lord, was an obligation laid on the wider group of all disciples. It was by the going forth of the word about Jesus – his life, teaching, death and resurrection – that others would come to believe, to enter God's kingdom through repentance and receive the blessing of forgiveness. Once again, as from the beginning, it was the intention of God to rule through his word and it was also the obligation of men and women to relate to him by believing it.

The word of God thus sent on its way came to be known as 'the gospel' or 'glad tidings'. As far as its messengers were concerned, they found that they had to bend all their efforts to making it known and had to be prepared for persecution. Its centre was Jesus as Lord and its central blessing was forgiveness. Those who believed in Jesus, however, were given God's Spirit as his presence with them from then on, just as had happened at Pentecost. The way to receive the Spirit remains belief in Jesus. No separate negotiations need be entered into for the Spirit to come; simply belief in Jesus is sufficient.

It becomes clearer, then, why one may say that Christ is both absent and present. He is absent to the senses and has ascended to heaven. He is present in his word, however, for to believe his word is to believe him. He is also present by the Spirit. When Jesus discussed his departure with the apostles he promised the coming of the Spirit and added that both he and the Father would, therefore, be present with them. Furthermore, the Bible not only calls the Spirit the Spirit of God, it refers to him as the Spirit of Jesus and the Spirit of Christ. In short, Christ is united to us in his word and his Spirit.

And yet the Spirit is not simply identical with Jesus. The unity of God means that he brings the presence of Father and Son, but he is not the same as them or to be confused with them. The Bible calls him 'another advocate' beside Jesus who is also 'the advocate' – but he is not Jesus. Indeed, in its language the New Testament makes abundantly clear what was still obscure in the Old Testament; that the Spirit of God has what we would call a distinct personhood within the Trinity – he may be grieved, he may be lied to, he leads, he may be quenched, he assists our prayers.

Nonetheless, the nature of that distinctiveness may be

the clue to the question of his role. It is interesting that the New Testament contains prayers addressed to both the Father and Son but not to the Spirit. And yet the Spirit's relationship with us is described in personal and intimate terms. But the Spirit serves to point away from himself. It is by the Spirit that we call God 'Father' (Gal. 4:6). It is by the Spirit that we call Christ 'Lord' (1 Cor. 12:3). It is the Spirit who inspires the word of God and illumines the mind to the truth of that word. The chief evidence of the Spirit's presence is not an awareness of the Spirit but an awareness of God the Father and God the Son: 'He will glorify me', said Jesus '... for he will take what is mine and declare it to you' (Jn. 16:14). When we see people listening avidly to the word of God, receiving it by faith in Jesus, calling Jesus their Lord and God their Father and united with one another in fellowship, we may be confident that the Lord is present by his Spirit.

To discuss or think about

1 What is the significance of Christ's resurrection? What implications does it have for our life in this present age?
2 In what ways is Christ now both absent and present?
3 In what ways does the Spirit bring the presence of Christ to us?

Conclusion to part 4

I began this section by describing an incident from the closing hours of the Second World War, not simply as a handy illustration of injustice in the midst of a yearning for peace, but because it is an indication of how divine and human concerns intersect. That is what our age does not grasp. Christian language is regarded as mythological, as having as little bearing on the real problems facing society as the story of Cinderella. It may offer personal support to those who need a crutch to get through life, but that is all. God exists in a realm all of his own.

Therefore, I spoke at some length in the beginning about our loss of moral framework. It is always easy for the moralist or the misanthrope to lambast the world for its follies and make everyone feel bad. Such words come cheap. I spoke of these matters, however, in order to show the immense present relevance of Jesus Christ to our society. We have lost our moral framework because we have lost the capacity to appeal to such categories as guilt and justice. Meaninglessness, individualism and misery follow. So does injustice and hence the destruction of true human relationships. But the work of Jesus Christ, future, past and present, shows us what true justice is about, and enables us to acknowledge the reality of guilt. It creates meaning, for it is bound up with purpose; the great purpose of God for the human race, the End he has in view. However, that is not all.

God's justice, his consistent goodness, has at its very heart, not condemnation, but forgiveness. Our world will not be helped much by the constant drumbeat of justice, guilt and condemnation. To have lost such categories is tragic; to have only such categories is disastrous. What we need is the consistent goodness of God. What we need is his forgiveness. What we need is that costly forgiveness of which the cross of Christ is both the source and chief example. Mere forgiveness without the cost of justice is sentimentality; it leads to a diluted morality. Mere forgiveness without the cross is pathetic. We are far better off with no moral framework if we are simply going to have either stern unforgiving morality or insipid amoral forgiveness. The cross makes all the difference.

When we see that God's passionate commitment is to peace with justice, however, and that he is involved with history, not merely sitting on a cloud above us in a timeless trance, reality becomes alive with his living presence. His commitment to justice connects the past, the present and the future for us and for him. Everything we say and do, all that we are, has to do with him. The considerable woes of our present century have been made a thousandfold worse by our incapacity to share his view on justice, guilt, love and forgiveness. The Christian message of forgiveness through the death of Jesus is a key resource for personal and cultural renewal now, as well as being our hope for a future of justice and peace. We can seek forgiveness only when we admit that we are in the wrong and are willing to repent. We can forgive others only as we see that we are forgiven ourselves, that for us peace has come with justice, that someone else has paid a massive debt on our behalf and in our place.

Forty years ago, Arthur Koestler and other ex-Communists published a book about Marxism called *The God that Failed*. Today all the world can see that the Communist god has indeed collapsed, and how 'a polluted civilization pollutes its own revolutionary offspring',[1] as

Koestler observed. It was, of course, a complaint of the Marxists that Christianity paralysed the political will of the masses by promising an unattainable utopia. The paralysed proletariat could not act to put the present right. It is the reply of the Christians that it does indeed take God to set the world to rights, and that it will be only at the end of history that he will bring his kingdom, but that his work is past and present as well as future. We affirm the present relevance of the gospel, not least in bringing true forgiveness into the world. In the next section we will see how our union with Christ works itself out in the good life that God has prepared for us to walk in.

My method has been to follow Jesus Christ in his future, his past and his present in the context of God's purposes for the world. We have seen that his future confronts our past and our present with justice. We have seen that his past consoles our fears for the future with peace and forgiveness. We have seen that in his present he is 'the man from heaven', as Paul says, the one who rules over this present age and is both the pattern for us now and our hope for the future.

In all this, the cross of Christ remains the supreme testimony of God's just and holy love. It was the most important event in the world's history. The worst and the best is now over. The praise of God for this great act will fill our lives for eternity. It should be even now the centre of our fellowship, our thoughts, our approach to God, our view of life. It means that we are not our own, but belong with body and soul to our faithful Saviour, Jesus Christ. It is, indeed, our only comfort in life and in death.

Isaac Watts captures the authentic note of a cross-centred Christian piety when he writes:

> Alas! and did my Saviour bleed,
> and did my Sovereign die?
> Did he devote that sacred head
> for such a one as I?

Was it for sins that I had done
he suffered on the tree?
Amazing pity, grace unknown
and love beyond degree!

Well might the sun in darkness hide
and shut his glories in;
When Christ, the mighty Maker, died
for man, the creature's, sin.

Dear Saviour, how can I repay
the debt of love I owe?
Lord, take my very self, I pray,
your work, your will to do.

PART FIVE

Life in two worlds

An angel of light and the triumph of moralism

Abou Ben Adhem (may his tribe increase!)
Awoke one night from a deep dream of peace,
And saw, within the moonlight in his room,
Making it rich, and like a lily in bloom,
An angel writing in a book of gold –
Exceeding peace had made Ben Adhem bold,
And to the presence in the room he said,
'What writest thou?' – The vision raised its head,
And with a look made of all sweet accord,
Answered, 'The names of those who love the Lord.'
'And is mine one?' said Abou. 'Nay, not so,'
Replied the angel. Abou spoke more low,
But cheerly still; and said, 'I pray thee, then,
Write me as one that loves his fellow men.'
The angel wrote, and vanished. The next night
It came again with a great wakening light,
And showed the names whom love of God had blest,
And lo! Ben Adhem's name led all the rest.
                                        Leigh Hunt, 1838

Here is a happy piece on the weaker side of nineteenth-century verse, but loved by generations for all that. For years it was learnt by masses of school children and, as adults, these children would recite it at social gatherings in the pre-television age. As you can tell, it is a defiant statement of religion for everyman, a sort of counterpart to the Apostles' Creed, a democratic version of Christian belief. Abou Ben Adhem may sound exotic by name, but he is as western as possible.

There is, of course, one puzzling feature. Who was this angel who interrupted Abou's slumbers, choosing his bedroom to be the scene of his midnight writing? Who was it to whom Abou felt the need to speak in a sort of antique lisp? Who was it that informed him that, by loving his fellow men, he had achieved God's greatest accolade? The word 'angel' means messenger, of course, and doubtless we are meant to see here nothing more sinister than an angel of the Lord. But, as St Paul reminds us, 'even Satan disguises himself as an angel of light' (2 Cor. 11:14). If we look beyond books of gold, lilies in bloom and great wakening lights into the quality of the message, a different perspective emerges. The advice of the angel was poison; it was a lie worthy of Dr Goebbels. And, insofar as it was taken seriously by those into whose heads it was so assiduously drummed, it corrupted and destroyed.

Mind you, I don't really think that it spread too much corruption. The poison was already present; the minds were already corrupted. Leigh Hunt's poem was enormously successful because it defiantly said what many inside and outside the churches have always believed – that God's approval is secured by decent human behaviour, especially love of other people; that all else in religion is superstitious mumbo-jumbo; that the real Christianity is a sort of God-endorsed system of morality. This has the added benefit of meaning that you do not have to attack anyone else's religion for, after all, cut out the superstitious god-bits and you are likely to end up with the same message, namely that God approves decent behaviour. This is the religion of the average person and it is the opposite of the truth.

God's way of salvation 'in Christ'

From the first, I have been telling a very different story. Hunt focused on what we do to win God's approval; the Bible reveals what we have done to secure his disapproval. Hunt's poem is on human effort; Christianity is all about God's almighty effort. Hunt congratulates the self-righteous; the gospel saves the desperately unrighteous.

What we have seen is that, although human beings repudiated God's rule over his world, God determined to re-establish his kingdom. With the coming of Jesus, and especially in his death and resurrection, the kingdom of God is asserted. Jesus is the new man, the last Adam, the perfect image of God. Unlike the first Adam, Christ lives obediently under the covenant of God.

The full expression of the kingdom of God is yet to arrive. While the old world with its sin and corruption continues, however, in the midst of its decaying life the future has arrived, and we may be part of it. We live under God's new covenant. For us, life in two ages, two worlds, two kingdoms is a possibility. It will of necessity be a life of tension, suffering and failure as well as joy, peace and forgiveness, but it will not reach perfection until God's future arrives in its fullness.

How do we become part of the future, members of God's kingdom? If the way of Abou Ben Adhem is simply the old sinful self-righteous way to destruction, where is the true path? Clearly what Jesus did on the cross showed God's gracious mercy towards the undeserving; clearly if Ben Adhem's angel is correct there was no need for Jesus to die. But, it may be argued, surely there must now be some human response, some movement towards God who has drawn near to us. Jesus died on the cross, it may be said, now it is fair that we repay the debt by co-operating in our own salvation.

Such thoughts, however, are only a little removed from the theology of Abou Ben Adhem. They still refuse to acknowledge how desperate is our position. They are tantamount to throwing a rope to a climber with a broken back and expecting him to clamber up it. They still fail to understand the sheer grace of God. The message of the gospel does not bring advice, it brings release; it does not bring law, it brings relationship; it does not bring medicine, it brings resurrection; it does not say, 'Do this to please me,' it says, 'I have done this for you'; it does not throw a rope to the helpless, it risks all to climb down, and tend him, and bind his wounds, and carry him back up. God is gracious both in winning and applying salvation.

The Bible has a special way of speaking about this drawing near of God: it says that those who are saved are 'in Christ'. If Christ remains a remote, historical personage, we can expect nothing from him. But he is the Lord of God's kingdom and he becomes our Lord when we enter it. He is the last Adam, and we become part of him when we enter the new race God has created. By saying that we are 'in Christ' the Bible is transferring us from our old allegiance to Adam and incorporating us intimately and securely into the Saviour and his future. We remain in the old age, but we are now also members of the new epoch of Christ. Jesus Christ is thoroughly pleasing to God, and we are 'in him', in God's loved one. There is nothing remote or impersonal about this salvation; it is union with Christ.

I intend to trace the way in which God brings us to be 'in Christ'. We will see that it is by his Word and his Spirit and that it involves genuine human response. But the Bible's way of talking about this never jeopardizes the essential point that salvation is by God's grace not by human merit. Of course, the Bible approves of right behaviour and character. But when human moral achievement is used to impress God and win a reward from him, it constitutes an assault both on God's grace and the gracious method he has chosen by which to save us.

Unfortunately, religion itself, including Christian religious practices, is often exploited for this purpose. Unwilling to admit human pride and incapacity, pride rejoices in religiosity and takes comfort from the fact of religious observance. Pride can exist in the simplest of chapels; it can be the very engine which drives the ceremonial of a grand cathedral. It can infect theology, liturgy, ethics, pastoral counselling, evangelism. Extraordinarily, it can be the basis of attempts to lead the Christian life.

The theme of this part of the book is God's gracious work of saving us 'in Christ'. It is also an exposition of the work of the Holy Spirit in the life of the believer. As God's pilgrims, we have not yet reached the new Jerusalem that I described in part 1. We live in the Christian life 'in transit', on the way, creatures of two worlds, and having to live in both for the time being. Many around us remain 'in Adam', associated only with the old way of sin and death. There are also many 'in Christ', however, who are looking for the day when his kingdom will come in its glory and power. In the first chapter of this section, I will explore how we come to be 'in Christ' and what it means; in the next chapter the subject will be our union with one another 'in Christ', for we are not alone in him.

CHAPTER 12

United to Christ

The blessings that God wants to grant come to us 'in Christ'. The process by which we come to be identified with Christ has two sides to it. I have called them 'God's open work' on the one hand, and 'God's secret work' on the other. Discussion of his 'open work' includes our own responses to him; matters like faith, repentance and conversion. We are conscious of the way he works as part of our experience and can analyse and describe it. To an extent, however, his is a 'hidden' or 'secret work', and we only find out about its existence and meaning through God's revelation in Scripture. Put together they bring us to Christ, or, rather, unite us with Christ. Put together they result in an extraordinary human freedom, which will also be part of this discussion.

God's open work

God's word
As far as we are concerned, God's work in our lives begins with the gospel which he has sent forth into the world. In its simplest form the gospel states that Jesus Christ is Lord and it challenges us to make him Master of our lives. It is a 'word' that comes to us in words. It may have come to us in a form that we can no longer specifically remember since we were so young when we first heard it. It may have been a word of complete simplicity,

such as a Bible story about Jesus. It may have come from a parent or a teacher. It may have come from a friend or a complete stranger. It may have come through a book, a film or a preacher. It may have captivated us in adult life. It may have been accompanied by an answer to a prayer to an unknown God. Somehow, however, we have heard about Jesus and believed what we have heard and this has been sufficient to introduce us to God.

Words are certainly capable of relating us to God. We relate to one another through language spoken and believed. By definition, we hear of Jesus Christ in words about him and, as we trust these words, so we relate to God. Words do not always accomplish this, however; they need to be both true and sufficient. We cannot trust a liar. We cannot build a relationship in an area of falsehood, nor can we relate where hiddenness or secrecy or obscurity prevails. Thus words about Jesus may fail to relate us to God. They may concentrate on his humanity and neglect his divinity, for example. Or they may deny his sinlessness or his temptations. The mere presence of the words, 'Jesus Christ', is no guarantee that the true Jesus is being presented for our faith and allegiance, even if we believe them.

Faith in God's word
In establishing his kingdom God has used words, especially in the form of covenant. It is by words that God relates us to himself. It follows that faith is the basic human response, for it is the very nature of words, especially words of promise, to be believed if they persuade us. That is why faith is such an important element in Christianity; it is the essence of relationship; it is a knowledge of God through the word that comes to us in words. Christian faith must not be confused with ignorance or credulity or superstition, as many suggest. It is not 'believing what you know is not true', or 'believing what cannot be proved'. It is not the opposite of knowledge, as both friends and

enemies like to claim. It is a certain way of knowing, a relational way based on words, the reliability of which may be scrutinized and weighed. It is a response to the persuasive power of the truth.

Faith as such is an extremely common human characteristic. No relationship is possible without it. In itself it is not especially noteworthy or powerful. It is not worthy of self-congratulation. Its effectiveness only arises from that in which we put our trust. Thus faith in the power of a rabbit's foot or other lucky emblem is useless; likewise faith in the power of the stars. Faith in an evil person yields some access to the power of that person but the results are twisted and infected. The whole usefulness of faith can be tested only by its object. Apart from a sort of placebo effect, immensely strong faith in nonsense has no power at all, whereas even a weak faith in the truth is powerful. The difference between faith and superstition is not in the mentality of the believer but in the object of his or her confidence.

This explains two leading features of what the Bible says about faith. The first is its exaltation of faith over good works as the means of salvation. If you think that faith itself is one of a series of good works such as generosity or truthfulness or love, the emphasis in the Bible on faith is quite puzzling. It almost seems as though God, having seen that we cannot do enough good works to save ourselves, has decided to lower the standard and insert just one, namely faith. But such a conclusion is a failure to see the unique nature of faith. Faith as such is no virtue; it draws its power from its object. Faith does not save; faith in Jesus Christ does save. Faith is relationship with God. It can be an alternative to good works because it is not, in itself, a good work.

The second feature is the Bible's emphasis on knowledge of the truth. If the strength of faith is measured by the power of its object, clearly knowing the truth about God and his ways is integral to faith. I realize, of course, that such knowledge of truth must be that fruitful knowledge which hears in order to obey. Nonetheless, growth in faith and obedience is related to knowing the truth, and this underlines the very great importance of the knowledge of the Scriptures for faith. We cannot know how to please God if we do not know what pleases him. He rules over us through his covenant which is expressed in Scripture.

Christian education is essential for the health of congregations and individuals. This must be more than a few minutes of Christian instruction per week. It must be founded upon and shaped by the covenantal Scriptures. A religion which prefers silence and private worship and sermonettes is really displaying a lack of understanding of God's gracious revelation of himself. It prefers its own thoughts about God to God's thoughts about it. Christian education needs to take into account the special nature of its subject matter and the need for learners of the Scriptures to respond appropriately. But there is neither excuse nor future for a Christianity which does not teach and learn.

Repentance

I have said enough to indicate that, if faith is the primary human response to God (since he comes to us in words), it is a faith which obeys. This is because the truth of the gospel has the capacity to change us as we believe it. Faith in the gospel frees us from evil and self-seeking patterns of life and remakes our lives; faith in the gospel leads to repentance.

Repentance is more than remorse or the gnawing pain of a bad conscience. Such feelings may reflect a true picture of ourselves, but they are destructive. To suppress them is dangerous, but so, too, is fostering them. Repentance, however, is healthy. It may be related to a particular sin or evil habit from which we turn away, seeking God's forgiveness and his strength to lead a new life. Even this is a secondary meaning, however. In the first instance, it is that turning away from a life of enmity to God which is also a turning to a life which accepts his kingdom, his rule. It is a revolution in attitude to God which leads to a life of obedience and goodness.

Faith and repentance cannot be separated. We cannot be saved without both. Our first step of faith contains repentance towards God, since by it we are abandoning our own self-regulation to turn to him. In fact, the gospel that Jesus Christ is Lord is a summons to trust him and to submit to him, to have faith and to repent.

Up to this point we have been describing the simplicity of coming to know God through receiving his word in faith and repentance. This is the basic truth, but three further issues arise: first, the psychology of the experience; second, the idea of conversion; and third, the nature of baptism.

Complicating issues

Psychologists have a legitimate interest in religious experience, including the way in which believers claim to come to know God. The Bible gives a sufficiently clear account of this to allow for classification, analysis and description. In the Bible's view, we generally come to know God through such artefacts of human culture as language and books. We are not at all surprised to discover that people and experience shape our beliefs. Our very prayers assume that this is so; so does our family life. It may well be possible for a psychologist to analyse a religious conversion with as much success as any other human experience.

A danger posed by this, however (and it is a danger to psychology rather than Christianity), occurs when an illogical and unscientific extra step is taken and it is claimed that the analysis 'explains' or 'disproves' or even 'validates', conversion experiences. God's part in bringing about faith and repentance cannot be reduced to the unexplained or bizarre elements of such an experience. Nor can it be simply discounted. It is God's chief way of dealing with the world and with us to use the customary or ordinary means which he has ordained, whether in plants, animals, humans or planets. You cannot locate his 'special' work, for he is in it all. The personal and relational cannot be reduced to the physical.

Some Christians emphasize conversion as the initial Christian experience, others baptism. Both emphases are capable of a distortion which obscures the truth of God's grace. Those who talk of conversion wish to insist on the personal, relational, inwardness of Christianity, fearing nominalism. Those who talk of baptism, and especially the baptism of infants, want to stress the God-givenness of salvation, its objective character, and they fear the undisciplined and harmful excesses of revivalism.

Conversion holds repentance and faith together. When a person who has been living without God hears the gospel, receives it, believes it and repents, that person has been converted. It is not a particularly biblical term, and it has its dangers, since it emphasizes the human will and the need for instantaneous decision and so may suggest that it is the good work which saves. As well, an inadequate spiritual experience (one not based on truth, for example; or one in which there is remorse rather than repentance) is sometimes called 'conversion' and becomes an apparent passport to acceptance with God. The result is presumption not salvation. Furthermore, conversion may be so overwhelming an experience that the experience itself becomes a paradigm for all spiritual experience, and others without the same style of conversion are dismissed as second-rate. This, too, endangers God's grace.

Notwithstanding these perils, however, conversion remains a most useful category for discussions of knowing God. It proclaims with bold power the need to make one's own the great obligations of faith and repentance. It repudiates second-hand, puerile religion. Many formal church-goers remain lost and unsaved because they refuse to be converted; that is, to exercise their own faith in God's word with repentance. They remain pharisaic rebels, without a concept of God's grace. Conversions occur in different ways; they may be instantaneous or drawn out, for instance. No pattern is the only right one, but of this we may be sure: no-one is saved without repentance toward God and faith in the Lord Jesus Christ. As far as we are concerned, if we wish to be united with Christ and receive all his benefits, it is by faith in the gospel and repentance that we come to that position.

The baptism of those who came to know God through repentance and faith is attested in the New Testament as being commanded by Jesus. It is a dramatic parable of the gospel message in which the washing of water portrays both washing away of sin and submission to God's rule. It is, therefore, an enactment of being united with Christ. The danger involved with baptism, as with any enactment, is that it may come to be regarded as conveying, automatically, the blessing it portrays, no matter what the faith and repentance of the recipient. This occurs, not so much because an automatic blessing is taught, but because the gospel of Jesus Christ the Lord, which is what baptism is meant to point to, is either not taught or not accepted. In the absence of the gospel, it is natural that church-going recipients should put their confidence in water rather than the Saviour. This tendency is encouraged by the prevalance of infant baptism disconnected from gospel preaching. The consequence is a fatal spiritual deadness far worse than the excesses of revivalist religion. To depend upon 'my baptism' is just as foolish as to depend upon 'my conversion'. Both attitudes are a species of salvation by good works. Like the call for conversion, however, baptism has its proper use (including the baptism of infants) when it portrays the grace of the Lord Jesus Christ and summons faith and repentance.

God's secret work

Re-birth

In God's 'open' work we are conscious of both God's part and our own. Lest we think for a moment, however, that our own part is meritorious or equivalent to a 'good work', the Bible not only indicates the weakness of faith, it also tells us that our faith and our repentance are God's gifts. Once again we notice that our own efforts are genuine, but that they are God's as well. We do not share them a part each; they belong to both us and God together.

We now turn, however, to what is going on in our lives as God's own and particular work through his Holy Spirit, for his gifts of faith and repentance flow from his dealings with us in a special way. The Bible is so conscious of our waywardness, or 'deadness' spiritually, that it considers that nothing short of a spiritual resurrection will bring us into salvation. We need to pass from death to life, from darkness to light, from bondage to freedom. We need to become new creatures, fit for the coming world which we are to inhabit. We need, in short, to be born again.

This phrase has become twisted and secularized in the last decade. The Bible regards it as the very opposite of human achievement. We are born again when God's Holy Spirit, whom no man or woman can order, dispose of or command, enters our lives and makes us fit to be members of the age to come. He makes the word of God, of which he is the author, powerful to our ears. He opens our understanding. He renovates the will so that it is willing to receive the gospel-word. He gives faith and repentance where there was only insensitivity. His coming is like that of a great flood of water on a dry and thirsty land and from his presence spring forth flowers and fruit in abundance. We could not do this. We could not change ourselves; we could not raise ourselves; we could not, of ourselves, want the true God. In the end he unites us to Christ and so to the whole life of God. This is what it is to be born again.

Passing from the old to the new is an instantaneous thing. We cannot be both lost and found at the same time, both in and out of relationship with God. Instantaneous though it may be, it is not yet complete. From another point of view, our re-birth is complete only when the End comes and we are physically resurrected. Being born again is, therefore, both an event and a process. In any case, it must not be confused with conversion, which is the work of both God and man, or, for that matter, with baptism. Re-birth is the cause of conversion; we respond in repentance and faith because the Spirit enables us to do so. Re-birth may precede conversion in time, for example, in an infant. In such a case the growing child will always respond by faith to the gospel and is never without a knowledge of God. To expect a 'conversion experience' of such a person may well be damaging.

Our choice and God's
Why, however, should some be born again and others remain in spiritual darkness? At one level we are operating here with the mystery of human choice. Even where a psychologist may be able to analyse human choice in this or other matters, our inability to predict behaviour with certainty suggests that personality cannot be penetrated from the outside by another human being. The Bible certainly praises those who believe and blames those who reject the gospel.

Something more profound is at stake, however. If faith is itself a gift and re-birth is the Spirit's work alone, the ultimate choice must rest in God. In fact, the Bible does not hesitate to say this. It refuses to tell us the reasons for God's choice, other than to say that he chose the weak, poor and foolish more than the strong, rich and wise. It refuses to let us know how many or how few are chosen, although its picture of the end of the age shows a throng of saved people from every nation, tribe, tongue and people which cannot be computed; it resolutely refuses us entry into the mind of God with the question of who specifically shall be saved.

Its purpose in telling us of God's choice, made in Christ before the foundation of the world, is two-fold: first, to bring down the last refuge of human pride where it may boast in the one good work of choosing God; second, to provide the one true base of human assurance, that God is saving his chosen people and will not let them go. In all this he is consistently good, for he has no obligation to save any and no-one has any call upon him, but he graciously saves those whom he will in his own way.

In thinking of God's work, open and secret, we have actually been travelling backwards from our own conscious experience. In our conscious experience there is God's word which brings faith and repentance, but we now see that before there was faith there was the Spirit of God; and before the work of the Spirit there was God's choice in all eternity in Christ Jesus. The reason for his choice he has kept to himself. The extent of his choice, except that it is a very large number from every tribe and nation, we do not know. The purpose of his choice was that he should have a holy and fulfilled people, reigning with him in the new heavens and the new earth. We now turn, therefore, to the consequences of this mighty work that God has done and is doing in our lives.

God's powerful work

Union with Christ means freedom for us. This bold claim may be regarded as nonsense by those who regard freedom as being the absence of external restraint, non-interference by others. For them even marriage, or the union of two human beings, which is only a faint image of our union with Christ, is an intolerable restriction of liberty. Since we are saved through submitting to Christ's lordship, how can this be freedom?

For our part, we repudiate such a shallow concept of freedom and reply that it is the very stuff of a miserable bondage to oneself. Its wretched individualism is contrary to our humanity, even in a life lived without God. It is a loveless isolationism – we are made for love and commitment.

There are three aspects to the freedom which is God's gift to those who know him by faith: freedom from condemnation, freedom from fear and freedom from sin.

Freedom from condemnation

Freedom from condemnation is basic to the other two. Whatever freedoms we may desire, including basic physical ones, nothing matters as much as our freedom from condemnation. We must all appear before the judgment seat. If we imagine ourselves there with any honesty, although we hope for mercy we cannot see how it can possibly be granted while God is a just judge. The Bible itself, however, contains a miraculous phrase which lifts our hopes: God, we read, 'justifies the ungodly'. To justify is to acquit, to declare innocent and righteous. It is more than merely having mercy.

This phrase is saying quite boldly that, against all our expectations, God has pronounced that guilty men and women are innocent, acquitted and justified. The biblical words do not and cannot mean that God has first changed our status as condemned sinners by fixing us up, making us such good people that he will want to forgive us. It means that, guilty as we are, he declares us justified. Our trembling, hesitant faith in him is not disappointed; it is met with acquittal, with justification.

How the God who says early in the Bible that he 'will not acquit the wicked' (Ex. 23:7) can say in a later part that he 'justifies the ungodly' (Rom. 4:5) can be explained only by an event which occurs between the two statements and changes everything: Christ's death on the cross. Here we have the condemnation of Jesus, the innocent one. It results in the acquittal of the guilty ones. If God, though consistently good, condemns the innocent and acquits the ungodly, it is because he himself was bearing the condemnation that they deserved. It is no wonder that the Bible must speak of grace; it is no wonder that it lays its heaviest assault on good-works religion; it is no wonder that true godliness says with the hymn writer, 'Nothing in my hand I bring, simply to thy cross I cling.'[1]

Freedom from fear

To be freed from condemnation is, in itself, freedom from our worst fear. But it transforms all our fears. It is a revelation that the ruler of the whole universe, and hence the one who is Lord over the past, the present and the future, is our Father. It is a revelation that we are the children of God. Physicists may still be in doubt about the nature of reality. The most simple Christian knows, however, that the Father is at the heart of the universe. We have no need to enslave ourselves to religious rules and regulations aimed at making us acceptable to him: we are accepted already. We do not aim at union with Christ through mystical and ascetic religion – we are one with him already. We do not need to use the uncertain resources of religion to ward off the dangers of an unknowable universe – it belongs to our Father and, although he may discipline us for our own good, we may be sure of his sustaining and ennobling love. We do not need to be afraid of the vast scope of all reality compared with our own tiny, obscure and frail selves – we know the Father. We are, the Bible tells us, heirs of all things; everything is for us and our redemption.

In particular, we are speaking here of a revolution in

the boldness and assurance we have in regard to God. The same Holy Spirit who binds us to Jesus enables us to call God by that most wonderfully familiar name, 'Father'. It is a constant reminder of our freedom from condemnation that we no longer fear to approach God, and that we have a bold and joyful access to the very presence of God at any time. We are, wonder of wonders, beloved prodigals, assured of our welcome, secure in the knowledge of his love, set free by what Jesus has done for us.

Freedom from sin

Our freedom from condemnation and our freedom from fear are realities, but also only partially experienced while we live in the two worlds. Our acquittal is complete but we continue to sin and so ask for forgiveness; we can never stray far from the cross. Our sonship is true, but the world reminds us of our weakness and mortality and again we need the assurance of God's love supplied by the cross. So, too, with our freedom from sin. It will occur finally and fully when we are in the age to come, transformed and purified, until we are at last like Christ. In the meantime, however, the process has begun; a process shaped by the cross. A true understanding of the nature of the Christian life must be built on the fact of where we are in history; between the ages, living in two worlds, subject to tensions, sustained by hope.

It is true that the ground of our salvation is independent of the good works we do, but the consequence of our salvation is filled with good works and with good motives and good character too. *Faith* is the pivot here. We are saved by faith alone, for that is the way of God's grace. The faith that truly saves, however, can never be on its own. It is, as we have seen, a repentant faith, a faith that places us under God's rule, a faith that wants to please God. Since it is faith, whose only strength is the Christ who died on the cross, it never tries to exalt itself and argue that God should be pleased with it and give it a reward for being so virtuous. It can only point to Christ. But, since it is repentant faith, a faith in Christ who died and was raised again, it never tries to laze about and presume on God's grace and live as it pleases.

In this present age we are progressing slowly towards what we will yet be. Many times our progress seems to falter, and it is as well to remember that an advance in holiness may simply reveal new areas of sin yet to be conquered, of which we may have been ignorant. The covenantal word of God with its injunctions, exhortations, wisdom, examples, precepts and warnings provides our guidance in seeking God's will. It will be found sufficient to lead us, for in Scripture is the Spirit's leading. In many situations there is no specific word of guidance, but we are left to use such wisdom as may be gained by the experience of being shaped by God's word and his Spirit. In all this let it not be thought for a moment that I am speaking of the private cultivation of a personal piety. The biblical material is relational and Christian piety is not spirituality but love; not self-centred but other-person-centred, with consequences not just for ourselves, our families and our churches, but for the very society in which we live.

In all that we do, effort is involved. There are no short cuts to being godly, no magic formulae or elevating experiences which will make life easier. Our effort for God will need to be genuinely our own. Having said this, however, we must again think of God's grace, and that in two ways. First, in his help. He does not leave us on our own; he invades our lives through his Spirit and we discover that any success we achieve is achieved through him. Second, in his forgiveness. Our efforts for God are essential; they spring, in any case, from faith, but salvation remains God's gift and, once again, we cannot stray from the cross. In short, our freedom is service, but not the service of those who must please in order to merit salvation. It is the service of true and restored humanity;

the service of love for which we were created; it is the service of perfect freedom.

It is a peculiarity of our time that the trivial secular view of freedom is found amongst Christians. We hear of an assured and present freedom from sickness, freedom from suffering, freedom from poverty, freedom from doubt, even, sometimes, freedom from sin in this life. It all shows a shallow acquaintance with the Bible and its treatment of the two ages in which we live at present. It shows a shallow appreciation of the extent of sin in the Christian life, a shallow appreciation of the suffering of Christ and, above all, a shallow appreciation of the power of the cross. It is the world in loosely Christian form attacking the church, and it needs to be resisted in the name of God and for the sake of true humanity.

To discuss or think about

1 By what means does God draw us to respond to him?
2 What is the nature of the faith by which we relate to him?
3 How do faith, repentance, conversion and baptism fit together?
4 Turning to God's 'secret work' in us, what does it mean to be 'born again'? Why are some born again but not others?
5 What are three aspects of the freedom which God bestows on those who have faith?

CHAPTER 13

United in Christ

The theme of this section is God's gracious work of saving us in union with Christ. So far I have concentrated on the experience of participating in Christ as though it were individual. This gives a false impression, however. As we saw in the first section of this book and have noted several times since, God is saving a people – a church, his chosen. In uniting us with Christ, the Holy Spirit unites us to God's people past and present. It is impossible to be a Christian without having a relationship to all other Christians, for all believers are 'in Christ'. Forming such a people is integral to God's chosen method of saving and to the End he has in view. In this chapter I will begin to explore the riches of our joint union with Christ.

God's saved people

God's people have their beginning in the word of God. The family of Abraham was related to God by his word; Israel met God and received his word at Sinai; Jesus called his disciples into existence and then commanded them to make disciples of all nations, 'baptising them . . . teaching them to observe all I have commanded you' (Mt. 28:19–20). The Bible regards Jesus as being the foundation of the church but so, too, are the apostles, whose uniquely authoritative words about Jesus set the whole thing going. In the vision of the new Jerusalem at the end of the Bible the city had twelve foundations, 'and on them the twelve names of the twelve apostles of the Lamb' (Rev. 21:14). The church is like a flock of sheep governed by the voice of the shepherd; it is like a bride obedient to her husband; it is like a vine in which the branches stay in place by keeping God's word. In all these pictures of the church Christ governs it by his word, having called it into existence by his word.

Continuous yet new

This poses the dual question, however, of our relationship with the people of God before Christ and our relationship with his people in the world to come. With the first there is basic continuity. Christ did not abandon his people when he came. They had been prepared for him and it was from them that the first disciples came. He did not found a 'new Israel'; he called on Israel to be itself. There is one people of God, not two. Christians are the heirs to all that God did with Abraham, Moses, David and Elijah.

On the other hand, massive changes resulted from his coming, as suggested by the parallel between the twelve sons of Israel and the twelve apostles. Before Christ, the people were a nation centred on a land and with institutions such as the temple, the law and the priesthood. After Christ, the people were international, and the fulfilment of their institutions in Christ transformed and spiritualized them.

The thing which caused most comment was the extension of its boundaries to include the non-Jews, the Gentiles. This willingness of God to include Gentiles among his saved people astonished the first Christians. They saw it as one of the most extraordinary acts of grace on God's part, since he had not bound himself to any but his nation, though, of course, the original promise to Abraham suggested such an extension of blessing.

Dispersed yet congregated

Understanding the present nature of the church requires an appreciation of her history in Israel and her future in God's new world. The nation of Israel was already, to some extent, dispersed; the people of God are now dispersed throughout the world. The nation of Israel has its capital in Jerusalem; the people of God has its capital in the new Jerusalem, the city from heaven which already exists and to which all Christians already belong. In particular, Christians, both Jew and Gentile, are joint sharers of the Holy Spirit, and the fellowship of the Spirit means that they are united with Christ on exactly the same terms and may call God 'Father' with equal boldness.

Here is our present relationship with the future. As I pointed out in the first section, the biblical view of the End is a corporate one, exemplified by the culture, companionship and love of the city. The biblical view, however, sees Jerusalem as already existing. Or, to put it another way, there is already one true church which is made up of all those who belong to Christ, whether alive or dead. We are 'congregated' (for the basic meaning of the word 'church' is 'congregation' or 'assembly') with Christ now. We are in union with him and with each other. The Bible says we are his body, so close is this unity. There are not many bodies of Christ, nor is it fractured and split. There is and can only be one body; the congregation in union with him, which we join when we are joined with him and from which we are never separated.

God's household

Its meetings

Christians form a family, therefore, whatever their national, racial or linguistic backgrounds. Our experience of church in this age consists of meeting with our fellow believers, seeking Christ in his word and relating to each other in love. Over the centuries we have added fixed times, buildings, liturgy, ecclesiastical persons and denominational structures to our perception of what church means. Such things are doubtless most helpful and they reflect and promote various aspects of the reality of our meeting together. But the essence remains the meeting of the Lord's people, drawn to seek Christ in his word and to bless each other in love.

In short, it reflects the union of Christ with his people and with each other. A Christian family will meet in church day by day at home; it will be no more or less church than the cathedral or chapel. It is not *part* of the body of Christ; it *is* the body of Christ. It is, like our regular Sunday meeting, a genuine manifestation of the one true church to which we all belong. Its title deeds and right to meet are the Scriptures which contain the promise of Christ's presence. Its history is the history of God's people, as is its experience, for it is often the case that believers and unbelievers mix in the earthly congregations, and only God knows who truly belongs to him. Church membership, even church leadership, is no guarantee of salvation.

Its structure

The structures of our meetings reflect their constitution. Provision must be made for the protection and nurture of God's family, and the congregation should have an appointed eldership. The central task of the eldership is the teaching of God's word by word and by example. There is an on-going responsibility for others who are in the care of the elders that is not discharged simply by verbal instruction. The eldership have an obligation to God to watch over the spiritual life of those in their care, whether it be their own children or a far wider group. In accordance with God's own rule, they must not be tyrants or authoritarian, but must rule in loving service. So important is this role amongst God's people that it is permitted that some be paid so that it can be done more fully.

The fact that some have a ministry of eldership does not discharge the obligations of the rest, however. The ministry of eldership is simply part of the ministry or service that all Christians owe one another, especially in the congregation, since all are united in Christ. All are called upon to be concerned for the holiness of the congregation and are called to admonish, exhort, teach and be examples. Our progress in godliness is never a private affair; it is directly related to our membership of Christ's body, from which we gain support. We grow (or fail to grow) together. It is here, too, that we have many opportunities for love in the way we treat one another. This applies even to the discipline for gross offences, should the need arise, in which the congregation as a whole are to withdraw their fellowship in order to win the offender to repentance.

The ministry of believers to one another is summed up in the word 'love'. We are to love our neighbour whoever that is. We owe a special obligation of love, however, to those who, like us, are drawn by the Spirit into union with Christ. Church unity is the maintenance of this bond of the Spirit. Love is the exercise of the gifts that the Spirit gives me (or their non-exercise, if that is right) for the benefit of my fellow believers. Nothing could be stranger in this connection than the current obsession with 'spiritual gifts'. It is almost as though they are being used as a way of reassuring the believer of his or her own identity. Their real purpose is for the good of others, and in one sense it would be better if our talk of gifts disappeared in favour of perceiving the needs of others and attempting to meet them in love.

It is interesting that the Bible does not use the word 'worship' in connection with our earthly assemblies. It may have foreseen the terrible consequences of a doctrine of worship which has become uncoupled from love. We meet each other in order to seek Christ together. One of the most bizarre beliefs in Christendom is that our meetings are satisfactory as long as they are an ornate, courtly, religious ballet and ensure that Christians are kept from meeting and loving one another. There is a vague memory of how we are meant to relate in the greeting of peace which we have now inserted into the liturgy as though this is a hygienic way of being friendly, a sort of sanitized version of love. See how these Christians love one another!

The Holy Communion, in the course of which we are now permitted by liturgical decree to shake hands, is meant to be a feast of love. Jesus ate with sinners and outcasts during his life on earth, thus proclaiming, in a strong and practical way, his forgiving acceptance of them. By his own words he ensured that a meal to remember him and, in particular, his death to bring about forgiveness of their sins, was to be continued by his disciples. We need have no doubt that the formal memory of his death was incorporated into the context of a meal in those early years. In eating bread and drinking wine, they proclaimed the death of Jesus. Through it they were reminded that their union with him was by grace, by forgiveness and, furthermore, that their union with one another was on exactly the same ground. Their participation in bread and wine was unity with Christ's death and unity in Christ's death. The union is so profound that you may even speak of eating Christ's body and drinking his blood.

What breaches that unity with Christ, what is an offence to his body, is the ill-treatment of one another. Lack of love between Christians is that which assaults the body of Christ given on the cross. It is tragic that Christian history has seen the simplicity of this meal become a source of hatred and discord, since it was intended to set forth the gospel message that Christ died for sinners and to confirm our union with him and with each other.

Its life-principle: the gospel of grace

The constant need in this, as in all areas of the life of churches, is to ensure that what is done is ordered by the gospel of God's grace. It is so easy for human pride to infect the common life of Christians and for their joint life and ministry to become motivated by the desire to do good works to gain God's acceptance. Whether our churches are liturgical or informal, whether our ministry is linked with a long historical succession or is merely recognized by a small group of fellow believers, all must be shaped by the gospel of God's grace, and be reformed where necessary.

I have said nothing about the church's mission for a reason. We can, in a sense, over-emphasize the church – which is not, after all, God's kingdom, though it is a consequence of his kingdom. Whether our fellow believers join us or not, we have an obligation to live under God's rule in all things and this includes the responsibility he has given us to proclaim his word. To say that this is the mission of the church is to run the risk that it will be confused with the task of its eldership, and that it will only encourage us to wait until we all act together. Certainly the church is under Christ's rule and, therefore, under his command to evangelize, but so, too, is every individual.

Nor have I said anything about church and state. In one sense church and state cannot relate for they represent different spheres of reality. Once again the danger is that the denominational church and, in particular, 'heads' of denominations, will be seen as those who can speak for and negotiate for 'the church', and hence for God. National leaders will be led to think that if they can appease or bully a denomination they have superseded the church and silenced God. It is better, once again, to point all concerned to the reality of God's kingdom or rule under whose provisions they govern and to whom they are directly responsible. The church can bear witness to the kingdom of God but it does not administer the kingdom and should not be confused with it.

To discuss or think about

1 In what ways is the people of God continuous throughout history yet transformed by the coming of Christ?
2 Why do we speak of the *family* of God?
3 What part do (or should) love and grace play in the life of the church?

Conclusion to part 5

Philosophers, and other mere mortals, sometimes think and argue about 'the good life': what constitutes the kind, or way, of life that it would make sense to choose. What is the best lifestyle? The answer tests our beliefs about values, virtues and purposes.

There are some who choose pleasure as the supreme value. It need not be sensual pleasure; it could be spiritual or intellectual, but this would be the goal of life. Others have a more 'mixed' approach, and would look for a varied life, seeking such things as balance, moderation, excellence, pleasure and even love. Such a view can be as elitist as the first idea is selfish.

Christians are conscious that our present life is, as it were, played out on the side of an active volcano. Talk of 'pleasure', 'balance', 'excellence' is hardly realistic. The 'good life' has been lived in our midst, and it ended in crucifixion. It is the nature of this end, however, which gives hope to the fractured, the sinful, the broken, the divorced, the sick, the deprived, the disabled, the abused. We, too, can live the good life and we, too, can reach the proper end of being human.

It is not, however, by following the angel's advice to Abou Ben Adhem. That is the way of self-confidence, of middle-class morality, of false and deadly comfort. Despair of oneself is the way of access: 'Blessed are the poor in spirit,' said Jesus. Every life is summed up by its final connection with one of two ages, two worlds, two ways, two men: 'For as in Adam all die,' warns Paul tersely, 'so also in Christ shall all be made alive' (1 Cor. 15:22). In Christ alone, beyond this present evil age, human beings reach their promised potential, have dominion over all things, and come to their fulfilment in love. Those who are in Christ will make their proper submission to God, and love will triumph in all God's creation.

The universe is a mysterious place. Physicists unwrap each riddle, only to expose fresh conundrums. Whether on the scale of the cosmos or in my personal experience there seems to be ignorance and darkness, black holes of the mind. We long to know what is at the heart of it all, to have some fixed point from which we can interpret our lives. The great French thinker, Pascal, said, 'Jesus Christ is the centre of everything and the object of everything; and he who does not know him, knows nothing of the order of the world and nothing of himself.' If we follow this clue, we find that at the heart of all things is God, and we find as we look on the face of Jesus Christ that this God – Father, Son and Holy Spirit – is love. The God who loves is at the heart of the universe.

Epilogue

As I finish this book, I am conscious of the foolishness of a mere mortal, and a sinful one at that, daring to speak about God. And yet we speak about him with confidence because he has spoken about himself. The mystical, non-verbal strain of much modern Christianity does not do justice to what God has done for us. It condemns us to doubt where we can have a joyful assurance instead. It reminds us, however, that our God is far beyond our comprehension.

The apostle Paul captured this dual sense of God's transcendent greatness on the one hand and his nearness on the other in the words which conclude the eleventh chapter of Romans. Having focused on all that God has done in Jesus Christ, he burst forth into a great expression of praise which provides us with a fitting place to conclude:

> Oh, the depth of the riches of the
>   wisdom and knowledge of God!
> How unsearchable his judgments
> and his paths beyond tracing out!
> 'Who has known the mind of the Lord
>   Or who has been his counsellor?'
> 'Who has ever given to God,
>   that God should repay him?'
> For from him and through him and to
>   him are all things.
> To him be the glory for ever! Amen.
>   (Rom. 11:33–36, NIV)

Notes

Introduction to part 1

1. D. A. Hay, *Economics Today* (Leicester: Apollos, 1989), p. 273.
2. Peter L. Berger, *The Heretical Imperative* (London: Collins, 1980), p. 3.

Chapter 1

1. Mircea Eliade, *The Myth of the Eternal Return* (Princeton: Princeton University Press, 1974).
2. Mircea Eliade, *Occultism, Witchcraft and Cultural Fashions* (Chicago: University of Chicago Press, 1976), p. 61.

Chapter 2

1. J. S. Whale, *Christian Doctrine* (Cambridge: Cambridge University Press, 1952), pp. 186–187.
2. Quoted in J. Bowker, *The Sense of God* (Oxford: Clarendon Press, 1973), p. 212.

Introduction to part 2

1. Sir Arthur Conan Doyle, *The Complete Professor Challenger Stories* (London: John Murray, 1982), p. 547–577.

Chapter 5

1. A. J. P. Taylor, *Essays in English History* (Harmondsworth: Penguin, 1982), p. 35. Taylor is highly critical of the total effect that this development had on India, though he also notes that the rule of the Indian Civil Service 'brought great benefits to the Indian people'.

Introduction to part 3

1. Thomas Hardy, 'The Dynasts', Part 3, in *The Works of Thomas Hardy in Prose and Verse*, Verse Volume 2 (London: Macmillan, 1913), p. 254.

Chapter 6

1. Mircea Eliade, *Myths, Dreams and Mysteries* (New York: Harper, 1975), p. 134–135.

Conclusion to part 3

1. Thomas Hardy, 'The Oxen', in *Thomas Hardy: Selected Poems* (Harmondsworth: Penguin, 1978), p. 229.

Introduction to part 4

1. Quoted in John Terraine, *To Win a War* (London: Papermac, 1986), p. 257.
2. Wilfred Owen, *Anthem for Doomed Youth*.

Chapter 11

1. John Calvin, *Institutes of the Christian Religion*, 3.1.1.

Conclusion to part 4

1. Arthur Koestler, *et al.*, *The God that Failed* (London: Hamish Hamilton, 1950), p. 26.

Chapter 12

1. Augustus Montague Toplady, *Rock of Ages*.

Index

One the whole, I have avoided the usual doctrinal words for the subjects under discussion, and the place where the topics appear is not always conventional. But the usual words are very important and should not be neglected. I have, therefore, prepared the following list which will offer a guide to where the relevant discussions may be found.